LESSON PLANNING WITH PURPOSE

LESSON PLANNING WITH PURPOSE

Five Approaches to Curriculum Design

Christy McConnell
Bradley Conrad
P. Bruce Uhrmacher

Foreword by Jacqueline Grennon Brooks

TEACHERS COLLEGE PRESS
TEACHERS COLLEGE | COLUMBIA UNIVERSITY
NEW YORK AND LONDON

Published by Teachers College Press,® 1234 Amsterdam Avenue, New York, NY 10027

Cover art and design by Rebecca Lown Design.

Library of Congress Cataloging-in-Publication Data

Names: McConnell, Christy, author. | Conrad, Bradley, author. | Uhrmacher, P. Bruce, author.
Title: Lesson planning with purpose : five approaches to curriculum design / Christy McConnell, Bradley Conrad, P. Bruce Uhrmacher ; foreword by Jacqueline Grennon Brooks.
Description: New York, NY : Teachers College Press, 2020. | Includes bibliographical references and index.
Identifiers: LCCN 2020010770 (print) | LCCN 2020010771 (ebook) | ISBN 9780807763988 (paperback) | ISBN 9780807763995 (hardcover) | ISBN 9780807778616 (ebook)
Subjects: LCSH: Lesson planning. | Curriculum planning.
Classification: LCC LB1027.4 .M37 2020 (print) | LCC LB1027.4 (ebook) | DDC 371.3028—dc23
LC record available at https://lccn.loc.gov/2020010770
LC ebook record available at https://lccn.loc.gov/2020010771

ISBN 978-0-8077-6398-8 (paper)
ISBN 978-0-8077-6399-5 (hardcover)
ISBN 978-0-8077-7861-6 (ebook)

Printed on acid-free paper
Manufactured in the United States of America

To our families without whom our lives would be dull and our writing duller still.

To the memory of Elliot Eisner (1933–2014), whose ideas we hope will inspire generations to come.

To teachers everywhere who plan with purpose every day. We hope this book unleashes your creativity and makes your work more meaningful.

Contents

Foreword

In an era of pressures toward standardization, it is easy to lose sight of the most essential components of education for all students: teachers and their pedagogies and practices. This timeless book is a timely reminder that it is the pedagogical knowledge and autonomous creativity of teachers that sit at the heart of the educational enterprise.

Lesson planning isn't neutral. Neither are any of the myriad elements of classroom life— resources found in classrooms, teacher methods of handling conflicts, furniture arrangements, or homework assignments, to name just a few—and a teacher's pedagogy can be witnessed in all of them. Are their multiple sources and media for information in the classroom, or is there one textbook? Are students working alone on assignments or with peers in conversation and interaction and co-production? Is classroom misconduct handled with punishments or through discussion? Are homework assignments extensions to or repetitions of classroom work? Or is there no homework? Do all students have equitable access to curricula? Teachers answer these questions through their pedagogy. This book centers its focus on purposeful lesson planning emerging from different pedagogies, but its advocacy for culturally responsive classrooms brings readers to appreciate a broad and holistic view of classroom life.

Analyzing pedagogies, trying out approaches aligned with them, and assessing student response and performance are parts of the process of becoming a perceptive, growth-forward teacher. McConnell, Conrad, and Uhrmacher raise and address these components of teacher lesson planning practices that serve the development of both teachers and students. They encourage teachers to unleash their own unique creativity, and they support them with templates for launching purposeful lesson planning that, in turn, serves to foster and extend the creative energies of students.

Our calling as educators is to guide students in developing multiple literacies on many levels. We seek to create classrooms in which we invite students to read thoughtful texts and learn to question sources; write interesting and persuasive prose and poetry; engage in aesthetic experiences and appreciate connectedness; see mathematics as a conceptual language; link history with the present; utilize scientific knowledge as a springboard for further experimentation; appreciate local, national, and global cultures;

and persevere in the pursuit of meaning-making. Our hope is that our students learn to search for big ideas embedded in the content we teach and the experiences we offer and to communicate their evolving thinking with logic, reason, aesthetics, and humanity. How do teachers skillfully plan to offer these types of settings? McConnell, Conrad, and Uhrmacher invite us to "come on in" through comparing and contrasting five approaches to purposeful lesson planning.

The authors provide multiple examples, reminding us that when a teacher's pedagogy is culturally responsive and includes social and emotional sensitivity, teachers guide students to finding learning pathways using links and materials important to them, while planning for "optimistic closures." With a pedagogy aimed at fostering aesthetic connections with objects or phenomena, teachers plan for interactive sensory experiences and encounters. When a pedagogy includes ecomindedness, teachers plan for opportunities to explore the interdependence of the natural and person-made world in which we all live. And, when a pedagogy is based on research on how students learn, teachers use student voices to guide the learning journeys unfolding within their classrooms. Pedagogies are based on understandings of human functioning. They are transformed into practice based on teachers' understandings of those pedagogies and their perceptions of the interplay between students' needs and the content under study at the moment.

Purposeful lesson planning is a core element of teaching. To catalyze teachers' capacities to plan lessons with creativity and purpose, the authors offer the powerful perceptive teaching framework, which proposes "Who I Am" and "What I Do" questions. This structure provides a grounded introduction to lesson planning for novices and a provocative reminder for veteran teachers to never stop asking introspective questions. The perceptive teaching framework helps teachers illuminate their own attitudes and relationships with the values and qualities of open-mindedness, awareness, caring, authenticity, personalization, intention, autonomy, and teaching the whole person.

With practitioner voices that recognize the complexities of classroom life, the authors advocate for curricular variety in classrooms and ask the reader to challenge personal mindsets, as well as the ideas of the book, in pursuit of making productive curricular choices from among varied approaches. The authors' reflective questions at the end of each chapter highlighting behaviorist, constructivist, aesthetic, ecological, and integrated social–emotional approaches kept me thinking, and their challenges caused me to reflect on several critical questions in my own work: Are some pedagogies subsumed by others, and if so, is it situational? Are aesthetic, ecological, and integrated social–emotional pedagogy separate from or embedded within constructivist learning theory? What are the teacher qualities necessary to maintain pedagogical autonomy in school cultures that try to standardize it? The book kept leading me to new inquiries.

The authors bring a robust background in aesthetics, and a focus on the artistry of teaching swirls throughout the pages. The authors invite the reader to blend the colors of lesson planning approaches to create new classroom curricula. Perhaps, over time, painting with new hues, tints, and shades, unique to each of us, leads to painting with whole new palettes. Education needs some new palettes . . . and some new canvasses. And this book invites us to pick up the paintbrush.

—Jacqueline Grennon Brooks

Preface

> Standardized teaching, from an educational perspective, is an oxymoron.
>
> —Elliot Eisner (2002, p.7)

Welcome to *Lesson Planning with Purpose: Five Approaches to Curriculum Design*. We invite you to take a journey with us along many pathways to engaging and meaningful educational experiences. No doubt you often hear that educators need to be more student centered; we agree. And we also believe that the experience of the teacher is important. Designing experiences for students and even writing lesson plans can be enjoyable, interesting, and creative. When both teachers and students are engaged in the educational enterprise, every day has the potential to be transformative. Whether you are new to teaching or an experienced veteran, whether you are an administrator, teacher–coach, teacher educator, university professor, or anyone involved in creating educational experiences, we invite you to explore these ideas with an open mind. Come on in! Let's explore together how we can plan with purpose and create unique, meaningful, and memorable experiences for all involved.

This book is comprised of eight chapters. We begin with an overall introduction, then discuss what we mean by *perceptive teaching*: our belief that you must know yourself and your students while cultivating culturally sensitive, safe, engaging, and inviting spaces for learning. We follow with five approaches to lesson planning: *behaviorist, constructivist, aesthetic, ecological*, and *integrated social–emotional* learning. In each chapter you will see five sections: rationale for the approach, theoretical background, practical applications, critiques and considerations, and a lesson plan for comparison. We want our readers to see that each of the five approaches has a strong research and theoretical base, and that there are many reasons to choose one approach over another depending on the content and the context. We believe teachers would do well to use each of these approaches some of the time: mix and match and blend.

The lesson plan example for each approach centers on teaching the concept of metaphor. We chose metaphor—or the comparison of one thing with another—because this concept is both simple and complex, which means it can be expanded in many ways. Further, we believe most of our audience will be familiar with the idea, as they likely studied it themselves. Throughout the text and in the appendixes, we offer other lesson plan examples from different content areas with the hope that all readers will see themselves in this book.

The lesson plan examples are written in both narrative and template form. The narrative is intended to serve as a think-aloud for the reader, to illustrate how teachers would think through the lesson plan creation process. The template is a teaching tool—a way for us to explicitly demonstrate the process of planning each kind of lesson. You will see a column dedicated to teacher thinking: This includes prompts and questions for teachers to ask themselves during the planning phase. In a second column we describe, step by step, what the students and the teacher are doing. While we believe these templates can be used to write actual lesson plans—and we have provided many such examples—teachers may also use any template they like or the ones they may be required to use. In any case, you will note that each template includes the unique steps for that approach. For example, the behaviorist lesson starts with an anticipatory set; the aesthetic approach starts with connections. While they are similar, we point out their differences and give some ideas about how to design this part of the lesson.

The final chapter of the book serves as both a review of the major concepts covered in the text as well as a place for extending the ideas. There we illustrate what blended lesson plans might look like when teachers draw on elements from different approaches. We also offer an overview of how teachers might incorporate ideas from these five approaches into an instructional unit.

Lastly, in the appendixes, we invited teachers to utilize our lesson plan approaches by creating actual lesson plans. There you can find lessons for teachers of various grade levels and content areas.

One more note: We tried to write this book with as little jargon as possible. When we utilized technical language, we provided citations for readers to look up the terms and the ideas behind them. Also, we use the words *model* and *approach* as synonyms. We settled on *approach* as our major term because numerous and varied ideas may fit under a given style of lesson planning. There are many ways to write constructivist lesson plans; we provide one approach.

This book is intended to honor teachers and the work that they do every day. We offer five approaches as catalysts for their creative thinking and in service of their students. This text is rooted in connection—connection between theory and practice, connection between curriculum and teachers, and most importantly, connection between teachers and their students.

We invite you to connect with us on a journey that has the potential to transform your classrooms, your students, and you, individuals who are called to do the noblest of things: to teach.

Acknowledgments

We thank the many people who helped us write and complete this book. First, a big thanks to Courtney Berry, Meagan Brown, and David San Juan, who wrote exquisite lesson plans for this book so that others may learn from them. Also, thanks to Sarah Biondello, who supported our project from the start and shepherded us through the publication process. We also thank our families.

Christy wishes to thank her son, Jackson, the brightest light and kindest old soul. She is grateful also for the solace of the desert and for the wildness of the mountains, where she finds inspiration and meaning and motivation to keep writing.

Bradley wishes to thank his wife, Leigh, his best friend and the love of his life. He also wishes to thank his special girl, Peyton, and his little buddy, Ryland, two of the kindest, most empathetic, and thoughtful kids one could ever wish to have. He is also forever grateful to his mom and dad, who always believed he would end up being a writer and always told him he could be and do anything. Finally, he thanks his grandma and grandpa, with whom he spent countless memorable and joyful moments throughout his life. He knows what a lucky man he is.

Bruce wishes to acknowledge his parents as his teachers for how to live, and he wishes to thank his grownup kids, Paul and Ari, who taught him so much and still do. And a huge thank you to his wife Lisa whom he loves, respects, and admires way more than he tells her and much more than she often thinks. Finally, thanks to Christy and Bradley, ever Lisa's children by choice, and Bruce's keepers of the vision.

CHAPTER 1

Planning with Purpose

The work of teachers in our time is demanding, often thankless, and always complex. So why teach? Everyone will have their own answers to this question, but we hope those responses include, at least in part, the desire to create meaningful educational experiences for students. This text will help you do just that, and it will also help you create meaningful experiences for yourself through the creative process of curriculum planning.

Teachers wear many hats, often at the same time. The perspective of this text is that teachers are curriculum planners. As Connelly and Clandinin (1988) have noted, curriculum planning is fundamentally a "question of teacher thinking and teacher doing" (p. 4). But what is curriculum? Oftentimes it is referred to as a thing: a binder that sits on your shelf, the standards written by the state, or the worksheets given to you by a former teacher. But we believe that curriculum is a living thing. In fact, we believe that curriculum only becomes fully realized once it is experienced by students. So that binder on your shelf isn't really curriculum until it is enacted with real students. Curriculum is a lived experience mediated by teachers and explored by students. Our text is intended to demonstrate how all teachers in all contexts can individualize the curriculum for students toward the aim of meaningful, rich, memorable, and rigorous educational experiences.

Here we offer five approaches to lesson planning: behaviorist, constructivist, aesthetic, ecological, and integrated social–emotional. Unlike many current trends in education that claim to be "the new best thing," we encourage teachers to use all of these approaches to planning as they deem fit. So, while some readers may be surprised to see behaviorism highlighted here, this decades-old approach still has merit for teaching certain concepts and skills. We also present in this text a cutting-edge method of integrating social–emotional elements within the academic content. This approach does not teach social–emotional content separately from academic subject matter, like many models, but rather teaches academic content through the social–emotional learning (SEL) lens. In this way the content itself—and the meaning students construct around it—is enhanced and changed by the method employed. But let's not get ahead of ourselves.

CURRICULUM LENS

This text is written by three people who have each taught real students in real schools. We have taught underserved students, as well as well-resourced students; high-achievers and struggling/resistant students. Today we are professors of education teaching these ideas to our pre- and inservice teachers. We consider ourselves *curricularists*, which simply means that we view educational endeavors from a curricular perspective. We subscribe to the view that curriculum is "a dynamic interplay between experiences of students, teachers, parents, administrators, policymakers, and other stakeholders; content knowledge and pedagogical premises and practices; and cultural, linguistic, sociopolitical, and geographical contexts" (He, Phillion, Chan, & Xu, 2008, p. 223). Curriculum certainly isn't just that binder on your shelf or that textbook on the corner of your desk, although both of those items could guide the interplay of the other elements.

This is a curriculum development text that will help you write daily lesson plans and unit plans. It is not an exhaustive text on pedagogical strategies, although you will find many discussed. A well-designed curriculum experience can mediate many concerns of novice and experienced teachers, such as classroom management, student engagement, memory retention, and relevance. If your students are "off task," we would suggest reviewing your curriculum to see how it addresses the needs and interests of students. If your students are struggling to remember concepts, consider an aesthetic approach. If your students need an opportunity to connect their ideas to the real world, try an ecological approach. If you are looking for students to develop self-confidence and social skills through content, try the integrated social–emotional (ISEL) approach. If you need to review skills like comma usage or the state capitals, try a behaviorist lesson. Planning with purpose will help you reach many goals for your students: academic, social, emotional, and more.

In addition to the curriculum being a way to meet a variety of educational aims, we believe such a lens provides a holistic way to design, implement, and evaluate the learning experience. We like to think about three types of curriculum: the intended, the operational, and the received. Together these make the instructional arc noted in Figure 1.1 (see Uhrmacher, McConnell Moroye, & Flinders, 2017).

The *intended* curriculum is what teachers desire to create in the learning environment. Current educational practices tend to use objectives here, although teachers can have learning aims in addition to objectives. The *operational* curriculum is what actually happens during the experience. Sometimes things go as planned, and sometimes not. Variances from the intended curriculum are often good—a responsive teacher takes advantage of teachable moments and can be flexible to adapt to students' needs and interests in the moment. The idea is that comparing the intended and the operational curricula can provide teachers with valuable information about their planning

Figure 1.1. The Instructional Arc

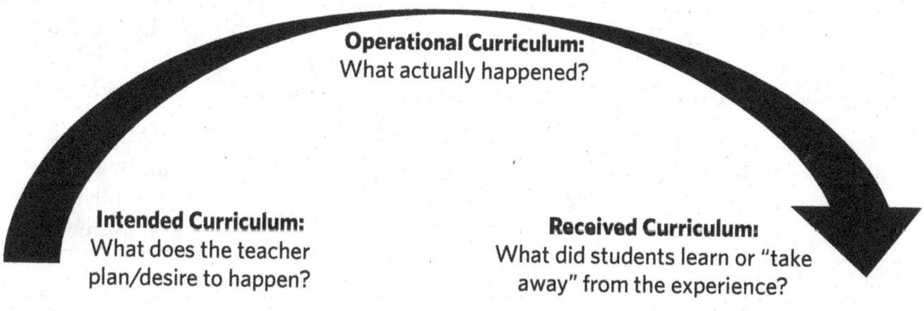

processes, student needs, and future experiences. The *received* curriculum is what students actually learn and take away from the experience. A teacher might intend to teach students to locate prepositional phrases, and along the way, they do! That is a good thing. But they might also learn something about each other during a paired activity, or they might learn something about their love of grammar or how well they can cooperate with people during a task. Together the instructional arc provides teachers and teacher evaluators with a way to think about and discuss how we plan, execute, and learn from our daily lives in schools. Further, the instructional arc can be used as a way to think about each of the lesson planning approaches we discuss in this book. As already mentioned, teaching is complex and ever changing. The instructional arc can be a useful way to think about what you want to accomplish and what students are learning.

OVERVIEW OF THE FIVE APPROACHES TO LESSON PLANNING

Our aim is to help teachers select, design, and implement lesson plans that create meaningful experiences for students while exploring rigorous and relevant content: to plan with purpose. You will see throughout the text that each approach has a different focus and rationale. Behaviorist lessons can be extremely helpful in initial skill development, but if used exclusively, the educational experience may become rote, dry, and narrow. So, as indicated in the overview chart (see Figure 1.2), teachers can think about their overall purpose or inspiration for the lesson—skill development; individualized meaning-making; sensory-rich, memorable experiences; real-world relevance and community engagement; and relationship building and holistic development—and then try out a format for that approach. These forms may also be blended, which will be discussed in more detail in the final chapter. Think of these five approaches to purposeful planning as your artist's palette. Colors are vibrant on their own and become interesting when

Figure 1.2. Overview of the Five Approaches to Lesson Planning and Their Primary Focus

Behaviorist	Constructivist	Aesthetic	Ecological	Integrated Social–Emotional
Skill development	Individualized meaning-making	Sensory-rich, memorable experiences	Real-world relevance and connections	Relationship building and holistic development

blended. As you practice each form and design lessons for your students, you will begin to develop a unique teaching identity that includes powerful tools for engaged learning.

GENERAL TIPS TO MAKE EACH APPROACH SUCCESSFUL

We encourage you to use this text as a guidebook. Take detours when you see fit, but do try all the destinations. As you design a behaviorist lesson, for example, you will note that taking time to write a concise behavioral objective with all of the required elements will serve you well. Once you identify the skill to be learned and the conditions through which students demonstrate that learning, the rest of the lesson should readily present itself. A constructivist lesson similarly unfolds once you create the experience that will then be labeled (i.e., explicitly identified with the students). Part of the fun of this type of lesson is the surprise and "ah-ha!"s you will get once the learning is labeled. We also strongly encourage group planning. In fact, this is how we designed many of the examples in this book. Our research has shown that some teachers even find co-planning with the aesthetic model to be euphoric—ideas and inspirations build on each other as teachers design the experience from the inside out. The ecological approach is also an exhilarating way to engage students with nature outside or with nature-based concepts inside. This approach may be of large or small scale, and you can design your lessons to be extensive or more efficient. And the Integrated Social–Emotional Lesson (ISEL) approach is a new way to think about how social–emotional skills help students access and create meaning around content. So, we invite you to try everything—it's a buffet of curriculum design, and you have paid for an all-you-can-eat ticket.

You will notice across all designs that we attend specifically to the beginning, middle, and end of lessons. While this may seem like a simple concept, we often see teachers focus heavily on the content or skill to be learned, but forget that an interesting beginning to a lesson makes the middle go smoothly. We also know that sometimes the lesson goes too well—or we over-plan—and we run out of time. So, we wish to reiterate the importance of pacing and rhythm in each day to ensure you pause for closure. Our brains love clean beginnings and clean endings, and attending to these will support your students' learning, regardless of the approach you choose.

Here are some ideas on the characteristics and rituals for each stage of the lesson:

Beginning: What signals will I give that the lesson is beginning? How will I entice students into the learning?

- Create and enact rituals and routines
- Create and share various types of learning aims
- Ask enrolling questions: HMOY (How many of you . . .)

Middle: What kinds of experiences can I orchestrate for and with students?

- Design the experience with components of the selected lesson plan approach
- Consider guided practice, small-group work and demonstrations, individual think and write time, gallery walks, and myriad other instructional activities
- Consider scripting your transitions while you become used to your new lesson designs

End: How will I bring closure to the lesson? How do we seal the learning for the day?

- Plan 4–6 minutes into the lesson for a closing activity. Don't just let the bell ring!
- Consider review and preview (big ideas, homework—oral and written responses about meaning-making)
- Include an activity that is compatible with the lesson design you have chosen

TEACHERS AS ARTISTS

We want to acknowledge the tremendous skill and artistry it takes to orchestrate a successful teaching practice day in and day out. As distinguished educator Elliot Eisner (2002) has noted, teachers conduct their work with skill and grace as they make countless judgments about the unfolding educational experience. Teachers must be innovative and improvisational in the often-unpredictable learning environment, as they cope with and capitalize on unexpected events. Lastly—and this is important—teaching entails attention to process as well as product. Through interactions with their students, teachers allow important learning moments to prosper, even if the day's lesson plan might prescribe otherwise. The artistry required for teaching well starts with a well-designed plan and is implemented by a strongly engaged, perceptive teacher.

To assist teachers, we draw upon our research as well as our work as K–12 educators to offer you the *perceptive teaching framework*. This framework reveals eight research-based qualities teachers can foster over the course of their career to ensure that their lessons will be received as intended by creating caring, equitable, inviting, and inclusive teaching and learning environments. This framework underscores the notion that as teachers, we don't teach content; we teach students. To really get into content, we have to create environments where students want to learn. This framework will help you get there, to make your lessons come to life in ways you can only imagine. Like artists, perceptive teachers have a keenness of insight, and this framework can aid in improving your craft as a teacher and as a curriculum writer.

WHAT DOES IT MEAN TO PLAN WITH PURPOSE?

Planning with purpose is about having intention behind all the experiences we create with and for our students. It includes being purposeful about the units we will explore in a year and the lessons we will teach each day, carefully sequencing and scaffolding them in ways that aid students in learning the curriculum. While teaching most certainly is an art form, planning with purpose also attends to the research base for effective lesson planning. Each chapter offers you an overview of the research and theory supporting its approach to teaching. Having purpose means being aware of why and how certain strategies and ideas work. This text arms you with the understanding of five distinct lesson plan models while guiding you through how you can create these lesson plans for any lesson in any context. Unlike a scripted curriculum, these models serve as a framework for bringing your creativity to life in designing learning experiences for your students. So what is planning with purpose? It is vibrant, intentional curriculum design done by creative, thoughtful professional teachers for the purpose of engaging their students deeply during the teaching and learning process. We invite you to join us in becoming more purposeful in your planning.

HOW TO USE THIS BOOK

Start with the chapter on perceptive teaching. There we explore why we use that term rather than the ubiquitous "effective teaching" language. Take time to reflect on each subsequent chapter by responding to the guiding questions and having critical conversations with peers. Don't be afraid to challenge or disagree with our ideas! This book has to work for you as a teacher. We do, however, believe that if you approach each chapter with an open mind, asking what you might get out of each variety of curriculum design, you will find useful gems in each model. You will also find several lesson planning examples, written by practicing teachers, in the appendixes. Feel free to use these ideas, but we also encourage you to write your own.

Again, we want to stress that we believe teachers would serve students and themselves well to vary their curriculum approaches. Certainly, you will find some approaches that you prefer, and that is a good thing to know about yourself. It is also important to know and understand why you might prefer a method—how do your beliefs about education, about students, about the purpose of schooling, and about life in general affect your curricular choices? What might you and your students learn from a variety of approaches to planning with purpose?

CHAPTER 2

Perceptive Teaching

Who I Am and What I Do

As discussed in Chapter 1, our text focuses on curriculum design—how teachers articulate purposes and intentions for learning, how they implement these purposes through the experiences they provide of the content, and how such experiences and learning will be evaluated. We refer to the types of curriculum included in this design process as the *intentional*, *operational*, and *received* curriculum. But we acknowledge that any discussion of teaching and learning must take into account not just the curriculum but also the context.

Teaching and learning is a complex, organic process situated in various contexts: the students' home and family contexts, cultural contexts, school contexts, peer relational contexts (sports, music, gender identity), and the classroom context. Students bring their life histories, cultural lenses, experiences, interests, and intentions into those environments. Before we proceed with exploring various curriculum design approaches, we want to look at the importance of knowing your students and yourself before you dive in to lesson planning. This is an indispensable complement to the lesson plan approaches you will learn in the ensuing chapters.

TEACHING IS NEVER A NEUTRAL ACT

No matter where you teach, how much experience you have, or how much curriculum you are "given" to teach, you make many decisions about curriculum before, during, and after a lesson, decisions such as:

- How should I prepare to open the discussion? How can I fit this video into the flow of today's class?
- What's a good follow-up reading or other resource to help my students relate to the class context?

What perspectives do we bring to all these decisions? As Paulo Freire aptly articulated, "Teaching is never a neutral act" (1970, p. 19). In fact, teaching is inherently philosophical, social, and political. We do not teach in a vacuum; we make decisions based upon various influences and beliefs, and those beliefs have consequences for our students and for society. Our goal as teachers must be to understand our own beliefs and the related decisions we make so that we can attend to the underlying political and social structures that comprise all educational systems in the United States. We must, as James Banks argues (2004), have a true multicultural literacy, which "consists of the skills and abilities to identify the creators of knowledge and their interests . . . to view knowledge from diverse ethnic and cultural perspectives, and to use knowledge to guide action that will create a humane and just world" (p. 291).

But do not fear! This chapter can help you unearth your own beliefs and intentions so that you can make use of them in planning your lessons. We do not believe it is fair to ask teachers to change society, but we do think teachers are agents of change for their students. The lessons and experiences you design can support students' growth, understandings, agency, resilience, and knowledge. We argue that the best foundation for doing so is knowing your students and yourself. This is the basic principle of what we are calling *perceptive teaching.*

To create rich learning spaces, we must attend to the individual students in our classrooms, to get to know them as people as well as learners so that we can identify ways to best engage them in the lessons that we teach. This type of teaching involves curriculum that is relevant to students, that challenges them, that scaffolds for them, and that sees individual cultures as an asset. Good teachers not only acknowledge students' cultures, but they invite them into the classroom; they are culturally responsive. Gloria Ladson-Billings (1995) acknowledges, "That's just good teaching" (p. 59). In the ensuing sections of this chapter, we will examine the qualities of "good teaching" based upon the vast body of research in multicultural education, culturally responsive pedagogy (CRP), motivation research from the educational psychology field, and our own research. We begin by examining the word "culture" in order to come to a shared understanding of what we mean when we use that word.

WHAT IS CULTURE? WHAT IS MULTICULTURAL EDUCATION?

The word *culture* has myriad interpretations and conceptions that range from race and ethnicity to foods consumed by a particular group. The *Oxford English Dictionary* ("Culture," 2019) defines *culture* as the ideas, customs, and social behavior of a particular people or society. Implied in this definition is that there is a shared element to culture among members of a group. Broadly considered, there are many cultural factors we might consider. One element of culture is a person's race and ethnicity. Gender, language, able-bodiedness, socioeconomic status, and sexual orientation all influence an individual's culture. On a broader scale, culture is influenced by people's geography, the groups to which they belong, the institutions where they work or study, their familial unit, their peers, their neighborhood, their city, their state, the clubs they belong to, the sports teams they root for, their religious community, and much more. Nieto and Bode (2018) define culture as "the values, traditions, worldview, and social and political relationships created, shared, and transformed by a group of people bound together by a common history, geographic location, language, social class, religion, or other shared identity" (p. 137). We can see that culture is complex, evolving, and cannot be essentialized; we must actively engage with ongoing understandings of our own and others' cultural identities.

We can think of our worldview as a lens through which we see ourselves and others in context. This lens is informed by our evolving and complex cultures and identities. Because so many cultures and identities affect how we view, experience, and make sense of the world, few if any share an identical cultural lens. Anthropologists Clyde Kluckhohn and Henry Murray stated (1953), "Every (hu)man is in certain respects like all other (hu)men, some other (hu)men, and no other (hu)men" (p. 53). Kluckhohn and Murray's point is that while we all share in being human, we are both a part of different cultures and at the same time highly specific in our cultural lenses. We must not essentialize or stereotype individuals, but rather recognize that there are many cultures that make up our students', and our own, complex identities.

To create an inclusive space where we are connecting to the whole student, writing meaningful, relevant curriculum, and engaging our classes, we must first grapple with and try to understand our own culture, become a student of our students' cultures, and create spaces where culture is viewed and actualized as an asset. There is a vast body of work on multicultural education that more fully elaborates on these ideas and should be a part of any teacher's working professional knowledge (Banks, 1997; Howard, 2018; Nieto & Bode, 2018).

Nieto and Bode (2018) offer three goals of multicultural education:

- Tackling inequality and promoting access to equal education
- Raising the achievement of all students through meaningful learning that provides them with an equitable and high-quality education
- Providing students with an apprenticeship in the opportunity to become critical and productive members of a democratic society. (p. 6)

These ideas are the philosophical underpinnings of culturally responsive pedagogy, which seeks to provide equitable, engaging, and relevant education to all students. We hope teachers will embrace a culturally responsive approach that provides an equitable, inclusive education when using our five lesson planning models. This approach is essential to maximizing the potential of the lesson planning models offered herein, and as such, we will examine it in more detail.

WHAT IS CULTURALLY RESPONSIVE PEDAGOGY?

Geneva Gay (2000) describes *culturally responsive pedagogy* as an approach to teaching that seeks to "empower ethnically diverse students through academic success, cultural affiliation, and personal efficacy" (p. 111). CRP is a frame of mind, a practice with a clear philosophical foundation seeking to equitably educate culturally and linguistically diverse students; it is not simply a series of teaching strategies (Bartolomé, 1994). CRP is an asset model that believes students bring unique knowledge, talents, and experiences to the classroom that can and should be utilized in creating a dynamic learning environment that is meaningful to all learners. This approach is highly individualized (Ladson-Billings, 1995), includes a deep sense of care on the part of the teacher (Delpit, 2006), and aims to empower students by teaching through their strengths (Delpit, 2006; Gay, 2000; Ladson-Billings, 1994; Nieto, 1999).

The definition of culturally responsive pedagogy is wide-ranging and somewhat abstract because CRP is as much a way of being as it is a series of educational decisions. Building on its strong theoretical base, new terminology and applications continue to emerge to advance the efforts of multicultural educators. Culturally sustaining pedagogy, for example, was posited by Django Paris, in an effort to resist a monocultural and monolingual society (Nieto & Bode, 2018). In our own research (see for example Conrad, 2011, 2012), we have found that culturally responsive pedagogy certainly gets us on the road to being better teachers. As we dove more deeply into this work, we began to look at the research in educational psychology, which itself had a robust literature examining how teachers most effectively engage their students. While this literature may not have been explicit in considering the role of culture in engaging teaching, it quickly became evident that there was significant crossover with what culturally responsive pedagogy researchers were finding. We collaborated with some of our colleagues in that field to draw upon our own research in perceptive teaching practices and to do a thorough research review and analysis of the intersection of CRP and educational psychology (Conrad & Shalter-Bruening, 2016, 2019; Shalter-Bruening & Conrad, 2014).

EDUCATIONAL PSYCHOLOGISTS' CONTRIBUTIONS TO MULTICULTURALISM

Educational psychologists have examined the practices of teachers who most effectively engage individual students (see for example Brophy, 1983; Anderman & Freeman, 2004; Perry, Turner, & Meyer, 2006). While this field of study may have somewhat different theoretical lenses, motivation researchers in educational psychology look at how teachers can create inclusive learning environments where students' individual knowledge, talents, and experiences are both valued and maximized (Conrad & Shalter-Bruening, 2019). In our examination of the research, we have found that the literature on motivation in educational psychology and the literature in CRP are extremely similar, save for different labels for analogous concepts.

One example of this overlap is illustrated by the quality of caring. The research in educational psychology points to teachers caring about students as being critical to motivating students (Juvonen, 2006; Moos & Moos, 1978; Solomon, Battistich, Kim, & Watson, 1997). Researchers have looked at how care influences behavior, academic success, attendance, engagement, and even emotional well-being (Barber & Olsen, 2004; Fraser & Fisher, 1982; Moos & Moos, 1978; Patrick, Anderman, & Ryan, 2002). In the CRP literature, caring is also a critical component to being culturally responsive (Gay, 2000; Lipman, 1995). Here caring is a necessary component of what Bartolomé (1994) calls a humanizing pedagogy, one that utilizes the reality, history, and perspectives of individuals in the classroom. Caring also seeks to create equal status while respecting and even celebrating differences, thus eliminating in-groups and out-groups (Banks, 2002). In this literature, caring is also linked to academic achievement, engagement, and self-confidence (Delpit, 2006; Ladson-Billings, 1992; Storz & Nestor, 2008). It is clear that there is significant correspondence between what these two bodies of literature have learned about the importance of care in the classroom. Our own research has found that care is critical to engaging students, creating safe, inclusive environments, and in being responsive to individual cultures (Conrad, 2011).

Taken together, the two bodies of research can provide a framework for teachers to create teaching and learning environments that are most beneficial in educating our students. The remainder of this chapter examines the qualities of what we call highly *perceptive teachers*, qualities that have the potential to greatly enhance the lessons you will create using the models in this text. Perceptive teachers are tuned in to their students' identities and their own, and they continually aim to reflect upon and improve not only their responsive practices, but also who they are as teachers.

Before exploring the qualities of perceptive teachers, we offer a few caveats. First, it is important to note that the elements on this list will not manifest the same way for every teacher. Teaching is a highly personal act that includes elements of one's own personality and style and, therefore, will look different for everyone (Jarvis, 2006). For example, when showing care to students, Teacher A may be more effusive in praise and compliments, while Teacher B shows care by holding their kids to high expectations and providing only occasional praise. We do not argue for one approach being superior to the other, only to illustrate that the quality of showing care can and often does look different for various individuals, even if the intention is the same.

It is also essential to articulate that the qualities shared below are not intended to serve as a checklist for teachers; there is no magic formula for teaching. While they are certainly valuable in helping us understand how to best create inclusive, engaging, challenging learning spaces, the qualities are not intended to be a how-to manual for teachers. Such a prescription would be reductionistic and disparaging to the complexity of teaching. Instead, these qualities offer items teachers might attend to in their practice and in their development as professionals. We must have a broad definition of quality teaching and cannot fall prey to a notion of "one right way." This is why we refrain from the ubiquitous and often misleading terms "effective teaching" or "best practices" and instead use the term "perceptive teaching." "Effective" and "best" connote a mechanistic view of teaching that suggests a guaranteed outcome if a certain tool is used. These terms ignore the significance of individualized contexts for multicultural education. We use "perceptive teaching" to imply the process through which teachers continually reflect upon, learn about, and adapt their teaching practices to meet the needs of their students as they engage in an exploration of rigorous and relevant content.

Finally, we would like to revisit a point made earlier: Culture is both broadly conceived and highly individualized. We warn that at times even the most well-meaning teachers may tend to inadvertently stereotype students. For example, a tremendously talented and caring teacher once shared with us that she had read an article about African American students performing better when working in groups rather than individually. She therefore had all her African American students regularly working in groups until a few of them informed her that they would like to work alone sometimes. That moment triggered her realization that while she meant to improve education for her students, her stereotypes overshadowed her students' individual needs. The approach to teaching espoused in this chapter calls for teachers to recognize, learn about, and attend to the cultural identities and individual experiences of all students, and of themselves.

QUALITIES OF PERCEPTIVE TEACHING

As previously explained, perceptive teaching names the process through which teachers continually reflect upon, learn about, and adapt their teaching practices to meet the needs of their diverse students as they engage in an exploration of rigorous and relevant content. The framework describing the qualities of perceptive teaching is the result of an extensive review of research in culturally responsive pedagogy and in motivation research in educational psychology. The framework is comprised of eight qualities, each of which has various layers. The eight qualities of perceptive teachers include:

- open-mindedness
- heightened sense of awareness
- caring
- authenticity
- personalizing the educational experience
- teaching the whole person
- teaching with intention
- developing autonomy

These eight qualities of perceptive teaching may be divided into two categories: Who I Am and What I Do. "Who I Am" includes attributes that are not always explicitly stated nor on display, but rather human traits that make up the core values of the teacher. "What I Do" includes qualities that direct behavior and interactions with and for students. Together these eight qualities when embraced and developed by teachers lead to reflective, evolving, culturally inclusive educational environments (see Figure 2.1). They help teachers plan with purpose.

WHO I AM: OPEN-MINDED, AWARE, CARING, AUTHENTIC

Open-Minded

Open-mindedness refers to the quality of being receptive and amenable to new ideas, situations, and people. A great deal of research has been undertaken in the role of open-mindedness in teaching, illustrating that this quality is in fact connected to good teaching (Garmon, 2004; Gay, 1997; Haberman, Gillette, & Hill, 2017; Shiveley & Misco, 2010; Swartz, 2005). Open-minded teachers are willing to try new things, are open to novel ideas, tend to celebrate differences in people, are willing to challenge their own assumptions and beliefs. Moreover, the open-minded teacher often possesses spontaneity, a willingness to go with the flow of things that might come up during a lesson they are teaching.

The open-minded teacher is also willing to take risks, to step outside of the known, or what is often referred to as their comfort zone. This quality lends itself to teachers being willing to assess norms, customs, or rules rather than see them as fixed, and to challenge them and change them when they believe it to be appropriate (Bennett, 2001; Sachs, 2004; Sockett, 2006). Moreover, the open-minded teacher evaluates issues that arise in the school or classroom setting through multiple perspectives to grasp a sense of a

Figure 2.1. Qualities of Perceptive Teaching

	Who I Am
Open-Minded	I am receptive and amenable to new ideas, situations, and people. I am willing to take risks.
Aware	I understand and reflect upon my own values, culture, beliefs, and practices. I actively get to know my students. I am open to feedback.
Caring	I believe all students are worthy. I build relationships with students and others. I create safe spaces for learning.
Authentic	I am present, genuine in my interactions. I am appropriately open with students and others.
	What I Do
Personalize the Experience	I provide multiple ways for students to engage with content. I invite cultural perspectives into the classroom as a part of the learning.
Teach the Whole Person	I view students as individuals. I support their academic, social, and emotional growth.
Teach with Intention	I make curricular and instructional decisions based upon my current students' needs and interests.
Develop Autonomy	I help students think critically, learn to solve problems, and become agents of change in their lives.

fuller picture surrounding the issue (Gay, 1997; McAllister & Irvine, 2002; Taylor & Wasicsko, 2000).

Open-mindedness can operationalize in myriad ways. For example, open-minded teachers are ones who attend a professional development opportunity with a receptiveness to listen and hopefulness to learn so as to improve their practice. When learning about a change in the school or district curriculum, these teachers refrain from indiscriminately rejecting the change. These teachers are willing and even eager to learn (Garmon, 2004; Gay, 1997; Haberman et al., 2017; Shiveley & Misco, 2010; Swartz, 2005;). That is not to say open-minded teachers blindly accept what happens; rather they will be receptive, listen, process, and determine their feelings and potential actions. However, they are flexible and resourceful with a belief in their own ability to solve problems (Boggess, 2010; Shiveley & Misco, 2010; Stotko, Ingram, & Beaty-O'Ferrall, 2007; Taylor & Wasicsko, 2000). The open-minded teacher possesses a growth mindset (Dweck, 2006), seeking to improve as a professional and as a person, a trait also linked to a heightened sense of awareness. Open-minded teachers are lifelong learners, continually seeking to grow as people and professionals (Shiveley & Misco, 2010; Stotko et al., 2007; Swartz, 2005). Further accentuating this quality, they generally possess a high level of perseverance, resilience, dedication, and stamina (Boggess, 2010; Gay, 1997; Haberman et al., 2017; Stotko et al., 2007).

Heightened Sense of Awareness

A heightened sense of awareness refers to one's consciousness of self as well as other people, places, and situations; it includes the ability to give careful thought to one's own behavior and beliefs. One with a heightened sense of awareness tends to be highly self-reflective and display a "with-it-ness" when interacting with others. Two specific components that comprise a heightened sense of awareness include self-awareness and self-reflection.

Self-awareness refers to the quality of being conscious of one's emotions, thoughts, actions, character, and individuality. This quality would include awareness of one's various cultural identities and how to navigate those identities in various contexts (Boggess, 2010; Fairbanks et al., 2010; Sockett, 2006; Swartz, 2005). Self-aware teachers are responsive to their students' cultures and are intentional about getting to know them as individuals, including their cultural identities, who they are as learners, their interests, their motivations, and much more (Castagno & McKinley, 2008; Gay, 1997; Germain, 1998; Ladson-Billings, 1995; McAllister & Irvine, 2002; Nieto, 2005; Sachs, 2004; Zeichner, 1996). Self-aware teachers are mindful of how others receive them, their word choices, their body language, and how they carry themselves. Such awareness allows teachers to stay in tune with their students, as they attend to students' body language, reactions, facial expressions, etc. (Conrad, 2011).

Self-reflection is the second key component of a heightened sense of awareness. While we often begin with an awareness of ourselves, our interactions, our thoughts, our motivations, and the situations in which we find ourselves, the teacher with a heightened sense of awareness is moved to then reflect on those aspects (Garmon, 2004; Stotko et al., 2007; Swartz, 2005). One must be both self-aware and self-reflective to be considered to possess the quality of a heightened sense of awareness.

Self-reflectiveness can take place in professional or personal contexts, and refers to the intentional act of thinking about and evaluating one's own thoughts, beliefs, motivations, or actions. The self-reflective teacher sets aside time to as objectively as possible ruminate on their thoughts, beliefs, motivations, or actions for the purpose of improving as a person or professional. These teachers are driven to be a better people and professionals while being willing to face their mistakes and self-perceived shortcomings

(Collier, 2005; Gay, 1997; Talbert-Johnson, 2006). They tend to be receptive to feedback from others and willing to process that feedback before sifting through what they might apply in their lives (Almerico, Johnston, Henriott, & Shapiro, 2011; Borden, 2014; Haberman, Gillette, & Hill, 2017; Tricarico & Yendol-Hoppey, 2011).

Self-reflective teachers consider ideas like their curricular intentions, the effectiveness of their lessons, their interactions with students, the results of student assessment data and their role in those outcomes, and much more. These teachers will often examine how broader issues such as race, ethnicity, gender, etc. affect the curriculum, the experience of their students, and the climate of the schools in which they work. A self-reflective teacher might journal, make annotations to lesson plans, talk with colleagues, solicit feedback, and welcome outside perspectives on their practice as a teacher.

Self-awareness and awareness of one's cultural identity has been identified in exemplary teachers in several studies (see Boggess, 2010; Fairbanks et al., 2010; Sockett, 2006; Swartz, 2005). Moreover, quality educators must have a self-reflective nature and willingness to modify their practice if they are to improve student learning (Garmon, 2004; Stotko et al., 2007; Swartz, 2005). Finally, in being aware of others and aware of issues of race, they must examine problems from multiple perspectives (Gay, 1997; McAllister & Irvine, 2002; Taylor & Wasicsko, 2000) while valuing, respecting, and empathizing with individual cultures (Castagno & McKinley, 2008; Gay, 1997; Germain, 1998; Ladson-Billings, 1995; McAllister & Irvine, 2002; Nieto, 2005; Sachs, 2004; Shiveley & Misco, 2010; Thompson, Ransdell, & Rousseau, 2005; Zeichner, 1996). In short, a heightened sense of awareness is critical to perceptive teaching and will support educators in successfully implementing the lessons that they write.

Caring

The quality of caring includes feeling and showing genuine concern for students as individuals and as pupils, which means that teachers care about them academically, socially, and emotionally both inside and outside of the classroom. In short, they care that their students succeed in school and in life. Much has been written on the importance of building relationships with students and caring for them. Nel Noddings's (1992) theory of care highlights the importance of teachers building and modeling caring relationships with their students. She describes a caring relation as being "a connection or encounter between two human beings—a carer and a recipient of care, or cared-for" (Noddings, 1992, p. 15). Others have detailed the need for quality educators to authentically care for their students as a means to creating an effective environment for all learners that encourages them to participate, engage, and connect to what happens in the classroom (Bennett, 2001; Bondy, Ross, Gallingane, & Hambacher, 2007; Castagno &

McKinley, 2008; Delpit, 1996; Galluzzo, 1999; Gay, 1997, 2000; Ladson-Billings, 1995; Lewis, James, Hancock, & Hill-Jackson, 2008; McAllister & Irvine, 2002; Talbert-Johnson, 2004; Taylor & Wasicsko, 2000).

In building caring relationships with students, teachers recognize the importance of respecting students while demanding it in return, which has proven to be a common intention in successful educators (Bennett, 2001; Bondy et al., 2007; Castagno & McKinley, 2008; Lewis et al, 2008; Thompson et al., 2005; Willis, 2009). Further, caring teachers are intentional about creating a safe environment where relationships may flourish (Castagno & McKinley, 2008). By building these relationships with and among students, teachers create a community of learners; this has proven to be essential to quality classrooms, particularly with diverse populations (Banks, 2002; Brown, 2007; Gay, 2000; Osborne, 1996; Weinstein, Curran, & Tomlinson-Clarke, 2003).

From an academic perspective, a caring environment can yield immediate as well as future benefits. Teachers who set high, yet attainable, expectations for students, while supporting them in reaching goals, often find that their students are increasingly motivated by this practice and are more successful academically (Banks, 2002; Brown, 2007; Delpit, 2006; Hernandez-Sheets, 1995; Ladson-Billings, 1994; Weiner, 1999). Teachers effectively illustrating academic care are more concerned with student understanding than with outcome or performance and encourage students to extend their thinking and apply increased effort in their work. These teachers clearly articulate to students that all of them can learn and be successful (Bondy et al., 2007; Combs, 1974; Davis, 2003; Haberman et al., 2017; Ladson-Billings, 1995; Middleton & Midgley, 2002; Sachs, 2004; Sleeter, 2008; Talbert-Johnson, 2006; Thompson et al., 2005; Turner & Meyer, 2004; Turner & Patrick, 2004; Zeichner, 1996). Through the enactment of care the teacher creates physically, intellectually, socially, and emotionally safe space, an environment that has proven to make it more likely for students to take risks and be more creative (Castagno & McKinley, 2008; Gay, 1997; Swartz, 2005). Care is a critical component to any effective teaching and learning environment and can lead to significantly better outcomes and experiences for students.

Authentic

Authenticity refers to the quality of being transparent and genuine in one's actions and being open to sharing one's thoughts, feelings, and true character with appropriate filtering (e.g., not swearing in front of kids). The authentic teacher is not drastically different in the classroom than at home, with a peer group, or with colleagues. Authentic teachers say things like, "There's not a big difference between the way I am in the class and the way I am outside of class because I feel like if I'm not living my life the way I want to live it at all times, I don't think I do anything in my personal life that is detrimental to other people and I would never do that in the classroom" (Conrad, 2011, p. 84). They tend to believe that if they are not authentic with their students, the students will see through any façade and ultimately be more likely to resist learning. As one teacher put it, "It's important to show kids your personality. It's who I am at home, it's who I am at school; it's me. They need to see that or they won't buy-in to me" (Conrad, 2011).

Teachers possessing the quality of authenticity do things like being open with students when they don't know an answer. Instead, they often treat such situations as teachable moments in which students and teacher can learn together. Authentic teachers are not interested in being perceived as all-knowing; rather they possess humbleness mixed with self-assuredness. They do not allow ego to interfere with the learning process but are confident that they can navigate unpredictable situations. Authentic teachers are willing to take intellectual risks, to fail, and to learn from their failures. In other words, they aren't afraid to be anything but who they are. In turn, authentic teachers are more able to build genuine relationships with their students and to encourage authenticity in them, as well.

Parker Palmer (2017) discusses at length the value of not only being transparent—or what he refers to as having integrity in teaching—but also the value of self-awareness in the process. He explains that teaching with integrity means finding a wholeness in one's self that is comprised of one's genetic composition, one's culture, and one's experiences, recognizing what is integral to selfhood, and then connecting with students by making one's selfhood available and vulnerable to them. Michalec (2013) seeks a way to bridge standards (the outer core) with who teachers are (the inner core). Moroye (2009) coined the term *complementary curriculum* to highlight cases in which teachers express their identities and integrity to their students. Each of the participants in Conrad's (2011) study access this complementary curriculum in their classrooms and believe that if they are not authentic, they will not be effective teachers.

WHAT I DO: PERSONALIZE THE EXPERIENCE, TEACH THE WHOLE PERSON, TEACH WITH INTENTION, DEVELOP AUTONOMY

Personalize the Educational Experience

A perceptive teacher personalizes the educational experience by recognizing that there are many ways of knowing and experiencing the world. With this understanding, teachers offer students numerous conduits to learning, showing their understandings, and making meaningful connections to the subject matter. Similar to other qualities of the framework, a vital component of enacting this quality is getting to know students as people and as pupils. Once teachers know their students well, they are better able to personalize the curriculum, to make informed pedagogical choices, and to help them connect students' interests and previous experiences to increase relevance.

The first requirement for personalizing the educational experience, featured prominently in the culturally responsive pedagogy literature, is *recognizing that culture is a lens through which we experience everything*—and we are always a part of numerous cultures. We cannot separate our cultures from how we experience and perceive the world in which we live. Teachers must recognize that students are not simply from ethnic or racial backgrounds, but they also embody gendered, communal, school, regional, peer, family, and other cultures. When teachers recognize cultures as a lens through which we experience the world, they are better equipped to personalize the educational experience and to teach the whole person. This becomes actualized through inviting students to share their cultural perceptions with them and/or with the class, viewing diversity as an asset. Teachers who embody this quality value individual cultures (Castagno & McKinley, 2008; Gay, 1997; Germain, 1998; Ladson-Billings, 1995; McAllister & Irvine, 2002; Nieto, 2005) while seeking to create opportunities for critical reflection, diverse perspectives in the texts covered, and space for individualized interpretation through various cultural lenses. These teachers see teaching through gender, class, power, and equity lenses while understanding that there are myriad ways to perceive the world (Boggess, 2010; Gay, 1997; Sachs, 2004; Talbert-Johnson, 2006; Villegas & Lucas, 2002). Research indicates a strong link between connecting content to students' cultures and increased engagement and learning (Ames, 1992; Blumenfeld, 1992; Kaplan, Middleton, Urdan, & Midgley, 2002; Ladson-Billings, 1995; Sachs, 2004; Turner & Patrick, 2004).

Along with recognizing culture as a lens through which we experience our world, personalizing the educational experience involves individualizing instruction and providing choice for students. Individualizing instruction includes tailoring the curriculum to students' interests, learning needs, and modalities; choice includes providing options to students when appropriate and possible (Gay, 2000; Tomlinson, 1999). Perceptive teachers know where learners are by continually talking with them and formatively assessing their progress to inform instruction. Personalizing the experience rejects a one-size-fits all curricular and instructional mode and embraces multiple pathways to accessing the content. This can be achieved by employing the various lesson plan models presented in this text; some days might call for a behaviorist lesson, while others would be enriched by an ecological exploration.

Teachers employing this quality rarely sit down during a class period, often confer with individual students, ask questions, push thinking, and pace their lessons in the moment. Some may have their students track their own learning to give them ownership of their educational experience. Moreover, this approach allows teachers to provide minilessons to small groups of students who may need extra support on a concept or skill. Others provide individualization and choice throughout the curriculum (Ladson-Billings, 1994; Storz & Nestor, 2008; Wlodkowski & Ginsberg, 1995). They do things like infusing multicultural resources into the curriculum so that students can see themselves in the learning while increasing their buy-in (Banks, 2002; Brown, 2007; Delpit, 2006; Gay, 2000; Ladson-Billings, 1994). They teach students multiple pathways to solving problems while encouraging them to use the way that works best for them.

Teachers who individualize the educational experience provide choice in what is studied, how they cover material, and even how long they spend with it; this is essential to creating motivation, developing autonomy, and providing ownership of learning to students. Offering choice over the curriculum, the learning outcomes, and even in how they achieve those outcomes has proven to improve academic achievement and problem-solving abilities (Deci, Vallerand, Pelletier, & Ryan, 1991). Choice can come in many forms for students, and teachers would be wise to consider the kinds and number of choices they offer, as limited choices can be much more effective than open choice. For example, a teacher might allow the students to choose which book they will read as a whole class by offering three to five possibilities rather than allowing them to pick from any book that exists. This approach is not only more efficient from a time perspective, but it also provides input and some element of control on the part of the teacher to have the students select from items that are in alignment with curricular goals. Beyond choosing texts, teachers might offer choice in how kids can work on an assignment, how they might represent their learning, or how they go about attacking a project.

Multiple studies have illustrated that students who feel a sense of control over their choices are often more engaged and tend to learn more than those who do not feel they have any choice in the classroom (Gay, 2000; Ladson-Billings, 1995). Because they feel empowered by choice, these students tend to put more effort into their work and are far more likely to persist through the challenges that inevitably come with learning; as such, they tend to achieve at much higher levels (Davis, 2003; Deci et al., 1991; Gay, 2000; Ladson-Billings, 1995; Reeve, 2006; Schunk & Pajares, 2004). Choice has proven to be tremendously powerful in motivating students and empowering them; we will cover it in more detail when we look at developing autonomy.

Teach the Whole Person

Teaching the whole person includes viewing students as individuals rather than just pupils in the classroom. When we teach the whole person, we help students academically, socially, and emotionally. Teaching life skills such as how to collaborate, how to overcome adversity, how to handle criticism, and many other skills may not appear in the explicit curriculum—or that which is formally written—but focusing on more than academic aims reaps benefits for student growth now and in the future. Seeing and valuing students as people, not just pupils, has proven effective in creating valuable learning experiences for students (Bain & Jacobs, 1990; Boggess, 2010; Brophy & Good, 1974; Castagno & McKinley, 2008; Collier, 2005; Gay, 1997; Haberman et al., 2017; Stotko et al, 2007; Thompson et al., 2005; Wasicsko, 2002). Those who teach the whole person are most certainly invested in their students' academic success, and they also strive to teach kids to be well-rounded, empowered, good people. These teachers will support students' academic, social, and emotional growth by offering encouragement, empathy, and resources they may need (Gay, 2000; Juvonen, 2006; Walker, 2008).

Teachers who aim to teach the whole person believe that their role as teachers is much grander than what might be measured with a standardized assessment. About her primary role as an educator, one teacher shared:

> It's teaching skills towards being a good person. What are you doing to make this world better or at least not harming it? Like thinking skills and learning how to be open minded and not automatically judge someone and just learning how to be open minded and learning how to express yourself effectively and how to get your point across. (Conrad, 2011, p. 250)

Similarly, another teacher who employs this quality shared that they are intentional about "teaching life lessons," seeing themselves as a "parental figure, teacher, counselor, and psychologist." Another spoke of the importance of helping their students "get the skills to be successful in life and be good people" (Conrad, 2011, p. 136).

Teaching the whole person very much connects to the quality of caring. In order to truly care for students, it is imperative to see the whole person, not just the academic/intellectual person, which is transmitted through both verbal and nonverbal language (Brown, 2007). Care is a necessary component of what Bartolomé (1994) calls a humanizing pedagogy, one that utilizes reality, history, and perspectives of individuals in the classroom. By knowing their students not just as pupils in their classrooms, but as people, teachers are in fact engaging in a different kind of pedagogy, one that is more than culturally responsive or humanizing, and one that is inclusive of all students.

Teach with Intention

Teaching with intention involves having purpose and meaning behind one's pedagogical and curricular sequencing and scaffolding, and requires a larger understanding of a students' future academic and emotional trajectory. From a curricular perspective, teaching with intention involves knowing where students need to go to be prepared for the next lesson, unit, or year. Teachers who align their instruction to intended outcomes while scaffolding their instruction to support students in meeting those ends have proven highly effective curriculum writers (Graff, 2011; Shulman, 1986; Stotko et al., 2007; Wiggins & McTighe, 2005).

Like all the effective teacher qualities, intentionality can manifest in any number of ways. For example, a teacher might look at standards at the beginning of a unit, develop summative and then formative assessments, before finally planning her minilessons (Wiggins & McTighe, 2005). Or teachers might complete all or some of the assignments they ask their students to do so that they can anticipate problems or identify potential difficulties the students may have (Conrad, 2011). Teachers may also identify models of past student work that current students can analyze so that they may be successful with the end of unit assessments. Intentionality may also look like a teacher focusing on the skills they want students to acquire and how they might need these skills in the future before writing learning targets for students. Regardless of how it is employed, intentionality is strengthened when teachers are explicit with their students about their process and thinking, which in turn empowers the learners to know what they are doing and why (Wlodkowski & Ginsberg, 1995). We will examine the notion of empowerment in more depth when we look at developing autonomy.

Teaching with intention also means selecting a good curriculum design for the content you are teaching. The text you are holding in your hands will support you in that endeavor. We believe that the five lesson planning approaches offered here may all be used by teachers to create a mosaic of practice—a responsive, colorful, engaging educational experience that evolves over the year as students grow and change with you. Teaching with intention means planning with purpose—we invite you to choose to engage students differently and actively by trying out different modes of instruction.

Develop Autonomy

Teachers who focus on developing their students' autonomy share control of learning with students, while teaching them how to think critically and solve problems. Like the Vygotskyan notion of the zones of proximal development (1978), teachers empower students to progress from total dependence through partial dependence to independence. In developing autonomy, teachers build capacity in their learners by helping them realize the tools of empowerment they already possess, such as being a strong verbal leader. Students then build on strengths as well as perceived weaknesses for the purpose of more fully realizing their capabilities. A strong verbal leader can be coached to become a persuasive writer with a powerful voice. Students become empowered when they are able to identify their strengths and weaknesses as well as when they begin to feel independent and successful.

When teachers develop student autonomy, students come to recognize who they are as learners as well as who they are as people, while fostering an increased sense of confidence in both. Teachers can draw upon their own positionality—their status as understood through gender, race, class, etc.—to develop autonomy by, as one teacher shared, helping their students gain a sense that their ideas matter and they are intelligent. In one study (Conrad, 2011) a White female teacher used her position as a person who is part of a system "created for white people, by white people to support white structure" to help her students navigate that system and succeed in it (p. 254).

At its core, culturally responsive pedagogy, and in turn perceptive teaching, seek to empower students to become active social agents of change (Gay, 2000; Ladson-Billings, 1994) and to help students recognize that they can, in fact, make a positive difference in the world. Further, building capacity and teaching for empowerment can ultimately lead to personal, intellectual freedom (Freire, 1970; hooks, 1994). Teachers should also teach dominant discourses, being cautious not to denigrate students' cultures (Erickson, 1987) while also engaging in difficult discourses surrounding issues of ethnicity, gender, race, social class, and power (Nieto, 1999). A large part of building capacity for the participants is helping students see the relevance of the work in which they are engaging (Wlodkowski & Ginsberg, 1995). Further, teachers maintain that their students are valuable and bring assets; this skill has proven to be an effective strategy used by quality educators (Ladson-Billings, 1995; Sachs, 2004; Swartz, 2005; Villegas & Lucas, 2002; Zeichner, 1996).

DISCUSSION

In this chapter we have explored that who we are as teachers influences all aspects of how we teach. Parker Palmer stated, "We teach who we are" (2017). By conducting our own studies and examining the research on culturally responsive teaching, alongside the research on motivation, we have discerned eight qualities of perceptive teaching: open-mindedness, awareness, caring, authenticity, personalizing the experience, teaching the whole person, teaching with intention, and developing autonomy. These qualities describe who perceptive teachers are, as well as what they do. We invite you to reflect upon the ways in which you can continue to develop these qualities in yourself and in your teaching. What does perceptive teaching mean to you?

Discussion Questions

1. How are you like everyone? How are you like some people? How are you like no one else?
2. What teachers have you seen modeling perceptive teaching practices?
3. What qualities of perceptive teaching do you already express in your teaching?
4. Referring to the framework, where are places you can grow? Where are your strengths?
5. How do the qualities of perceptive teachers help in writing your lessons?
6. How do the qualities of perceptive teachers help in implementing your lessons?
7. What is one quality you could focus on developing this day, this week, or this year?

CHAPTER 3

The Behaviorist Approach to Lesson Planning

Skill Development

The first two chapters have set the foundation for what is to come: five approaches to lesson design. We start with the behaviorist approach because it is likely familiar, at least in part, to many. Terms like "guided practice" and "direct instruction" are ubiquitous in contemporary education, but they have a specific and intentional origin that might be overlooked or misunderstood. Let's dive in to learn more about the rationale, background, and possible uses of this lesson design.

The behaviorist approach to lesson planning requires that teachers begin by identifying specific objectives or standards before designing a lesson that will help achieve those ends. This approach is considered "teacher driven" and generally seen to be successful based on observable changes in student behavior aligned with the specified objectives (Hunter, 1983; Tyler, 1949). Though historically the desired behaviors to be addressed in a lesson might be conceived of more generally, contemporary interpretations of behaviorism along with the general understandings of how to connect standards to the curriculum have led the practice of using objectives to be much more specific (Hlebowitsh, 2013). In its current use, a behaviorist lesson plan typically includes drill and practice, guided as well as independent reinforcement activities, and learning through direct instruction. Unlike other approaches to lesson planning, the behaviorist approach promotes the notion that meaning-making is separate from one's personal experience (Weegar & Pacis, 2012).

RATIONALE

When using the behaviorist approach to lesson planning, teachers tend to ask: What activities might students perform in order to meet the learning objective? This type of lesson provides an efficient way to teach skills and introductory content that might be needed for future complex and higher-order thinking. The class examines and practices ideas and skills as a whole;

all students tend to be learning the same content at the same time. The teacher is typically directing step-by-step learning with opportunities for practice along the way.

THEORETICAL BACKGROUND

Behaviorism in curriculum design has its roots in educational psychology. Researchers such as Pavlov and Watson laid the groundwork for it in learning theory, before it was ultimately applied in schooling. The central idea influencing behaviorism lies in conditioning theory, which explains learning in terms of environmental events. Conditioning theory says that behaviors are changed when a stimulus is applied or given to a learner. For example, if a student works diligently on a math assignment and gets 10 out of 10 correct and, as a result, receives a sticker on their paper, over time, that student is likely to continue the behavior of working diligently on math tests.

The theory known as operant conditioning, developed by B. F. Skinner, has been applied to many aspects of schooling, including learning and discipline, child development, social behaviors, language acquisition, and others (Schunk, 2016). For Skinner, learning was the process of changing responses in complex situations. Such behavioral responses could be reinforced—or conditioned—by certain environmental factors or stimuli. For example, if a teacher asks a question (the stimulus), Elijah raises his hand (the response), he is called on and praised for his answer (reinforcing stimulus). And while behaviorism as a learning theory is much more complex (see Schunk, 2016), we can see how Skinner's ideas of behavioral change have become prevalent in schooling. Behaviorists focus upon observable events that are evident once the teacher sets the proper stimuli in the environment.

Behaviorists acknowledge that internal events like thoughts and feelings occur, but they hold that these events are not needed to explain behavior or learning. Instead, behaviorism supposes that humans are shaped by their environment, rather than by free will (Sadker & Zittleman, 2016). If one wishes to change thoughts and behavior, then one must alter the environment. In the classroom context, teachers can alter the environment in a number of ways, including through the experiences they create for their students in their lesson plans.

PRACTICAL APPLICATION: LESSON PLAN FORMATS

While cognitive theories are more influential in contemporary educational psychology, behaviorism is still prevalent in schooling (Ellis & Bond, 2016). How does such a theory of learning translate into lesson planning?

A number of behaviorist lesson plan models exist, many of which are not frameworks for teacher-created lessons (such as the one we provide below), but rather have been pre-scripted for teachers. Examples of this abound and include *Everyday Math*, *Aim for Algebra*, and *Words Their Way*. In considering frameworks for teacher-created curriculum, the primary method of behaviorist lesson planning can be traced to Madeline Hunter (1983). Her book *Teach More—Faster!* (1967) begins with a confident statement about learning: "There ought to be some way to make this job of teaching easier and more predictably successful. There is!"

Her methods, called the "Seven-Step Lesson" or the "Elements of Effective Instruction," became so popular in the 1970s and 1980s that they dominated teacher preparation and development programs, in some cases being adopted by districts for teacher assessment and promotion (Hlebowitsh, 2001). The Hunter model lists seven specific, sequential elements of the lesson plan:

1. Anticipatory set
2. Objective and purpose
3. Input/direct instruction
4. Modeling
5. Checking for understanding
6. Guided practice
7. Independent practice

So how can the Hunter model help teachers educate their students? As Hunter suggested, on occasions in which the goal of learning is efficiency and skill attainment, the behaviorist model may be a great choice. Some examples include comma rules, finding the area of a triangle, proper running technique, safety procedures in a lab experiment, and other skill-based content that can be modeled, practiced, and mastered.

Contemporary instructional strategies like "explicit teaching" or "direct instruction" are rooted in behaviorism. Often such models aim to move students deliberately through a step-by-step learning sequence. Examples of this didactic approach include minilectures, guided presentations, storytelling, and demonstrations. Specific models of direct instruction such as the Direct Instruction System for Teaching Arithmetic and Reading (DISTAR) are also widely used in classrooms where behaviorist approaches to learning take place (Rosenshine, 2008).

One contemporary example of a modified behaviorist instructional strategy is the "I do-We do-You do" model (see Pearson & Gallagher, 1983; Fisher & Frey, 2013), which stands as a prominent example of behaviorist instructional strategies. In this case, teachers perform the desired behavior, such as finding the area of a triangle; students work as a class or group to find the area of a triangle; and then students work individually to find the area of a triangle. Along the way, the teacher can monitor for common misunderstandings and errors. As with the Hunter model, such a process is valued for its efficiency and overt demonstration of fuller, more in-depth skill development.

LEARNING AIMS: BEHAVIORAL OBJECTIVES WITH ABCD FORMAT

How then do teachers go about writing a behaviorist lesson? First, teachers must consider what specific behaviors or skills they want their students to learn. Then they must consider what acceptable forms of evidence, or assessments, they can give to the students to evaluate whether or not they have learned the behavior or skill. To facilitate the relationship between the content taught and the assessment, teachers have been encouraged to write behavioral objectives. Such statements are to include the Audience, Behavior, Conditions, and Degree (ABCD) to which the student must perform. We see here the connections to Skinner's ideas.

Writing the behavioral objective prior to the lesson guides the lesson structure. If the teacher identifies the objective as "The students will be able to correctly insert commas into ten pre-written sentences with 85% accuracy," they will design their lesson plan accordingly.

On the following pages, let's look at what they might do, following Hunter's seven steps.

ABCD Objectives

The *Audience* is generally the students.

The students will be able to . . .

The *Behavior* is the observable skill or concept the students are learning. It's the "what?" of the objective.

. . . correctly insert commas . . .

Conditions refers to the context for the behavior. It is the "how" of the objective. How will they illustrate, in a way teachers can assess, that they learned the Behavior?

. . . into 10 pre-written sentences . . .

Degree is the level of accuracy required to complete the assessment successfully. This is the level at which the students illustrate they have learned the Behavior satisfactorily.

. . . with 85% accuracy.

1. ***Anticipatory Set:*** Get students' attention and focus learning. The anticipatory set is intended to be a short activity, somewhere between 5 and 10 minutes, that serves as a hook for the students into the content that will be covered. Anticipatory sets may or may not be used as preassessments and can double as a classroom management technique designed to help students transition from a previous activity or, in middle and high school settings, another place. In a lesson about commas, the anticipatory set might look like this:
   a. Read a sentence out loud and ask students to raise their hands where commas should go. Repeat with several sentences related to their interests.
   b. Ask students, "How many comma rules do you think there are?" Elicit responses, which will be large numbers. Explain that there are only six rules they will need to learn.
2. ***Objective and Purpose:*** State the learning objective(s) and the reasons we need commas. They help us clarify and communicate precisely. The objective and purpose provide clarity and relevance for students, which in turn can increase engagement. Examples of objective and purpose in this lesson would be:
   a. "The students will be able to correctly insert commas into 10 pre-written sentences with 85% accuracy." This may be written on the board and read aloud by teachers and students.
   b. Ask: Why is it important to use commas? Put the following example on the board and ask which sentence Grandmother might prefer.
      i. It is time to eat, Grandmother!
      ii. It is time to eat Grandmother!
3. ***Input/Direct Instruction:*** Provide information that students need to meet the objective. Here teachers can draw upon some of the examples of direct instruction from this chapter or from other such sources. Continuing with our example:
   a. Put Rule 1 on the board or PowerPoint: In a series with three or more terms with a single conjunction, use a comma after each term except the last.
   b. Give examples:
      i. I went to Target and bought toilet paper, puppy food, and a birthday card.
      ii. Summer break includes the months of June, July, and August.
      iii. Summer break does not include October, November, or December.
      iv. For homework tonight read 30 pages, write one paragraph, and solve six math problems.
4. ***Modeling:*** The teacher shows the students the process or skill, trying to anticipate errors and how to correct them ("I do"). Modeling makes

clear to the students what is expected of them while allowing them to see what it is that they are learning. For our comma lesson:

   a. Write "I have yellow chocolate and black Labradors." Ask the students to volunteer to insert commas to show that you have three dogs. They may often forget the comma before the conjunction (the Oxford comma), so the teacher must reinforce that one.
   b. Continue with other examples, and potentially ask students to create one for the class to solve.

5. ***Check for Understanding:*** During the modeling phase, the teacher takes note of how many students understand the skill or knowledge being taught. Teachers can do this by eliciting questions, posing questions to individual students or the whole group, having students respond to questions on a whiteboard, or using technology to elicit replies to questions designed to check for understanding. Teachers can use any number of questioning strategies when checking for understanding. For our comma lesson:
   a. While modeling, call on students who volunteer, and also randomly call on students. Support all through their identification of correct comma placement.
6. ***Guided Practice:*** The teacher provides practice problems for the skills being taught ("We do"). Here the students begin to apply what they learned from direct instruction while the teacher guides them through the process, formatively assessing, asking questions, and/or extending students' thinking. The guided practice for our comma lesson might look like this:
   a. Put five sentences on the board that need but are missing commas in a series. Circulate as students work through these on their own.
   b. Put five sentences on the board that have some commas inserted but need corrections or additions. Be sure the only comma corrections needed are commas in a series.
7. ***Independent Practice:*** Students work independently toward mastery. This is often done as homework ("You do"). Now that the teacher has assured that students understand the content, the students can work with that content largely without guidance. In the comma lesson:
   a. Give students a handout similar to the class exercise to complete for homework.
   b. For each of the six comma rules, repeat the above process.
8. ***Closure and Evaluation:*** Although not a part of Hunter's original model, we include it as an important step. Here teachers focus on wrapping up and providing a review. Closure and evaluation come at the end of the lesson and is a brief (3–5-minute) window where the teacher reviews and wraps up what has been covered in the lesson. This final step is where teachers do one last check for understanding. Closure in our comma lesson plan might look like this:

a. Review comma rule 1.
b. Revisit the objective and discuss that students can now put commas in a series appropriately.
c. On an exit slip, ask the students to write where they should place commas in a series.

ASSESSMENT AND EVALUATION

Because the behaviorist approach emphasizes observable, measurable behavior change, teachers must consider prior to writing their lesson plans what can be assessed and how. Because the focus is on what the teacher can see and measure, the assessments must elicit such evidence. If the content taught includes, as it did in our example, the comma rules, then the teacher would need to create an assessment on which students can demonstrate their mastery of such knowledge. Assessments can take any number of forms, including traditional or authentic approaches, and seek to individually assess students' understanding of the content covered (Weegar & Pacis, 2012). The key is that the assessment is predicated on the specified objective. The teacher has already stated the conditions for demonstrating behavioral change, which determines what assessment will be used for that lesson.

CLASSROOM INTERACTIONS AND ROLES

The behaviorist approach puts content and learning objectives at the core of the learning environment. The primary result of the lesson is behavior change, directed by the teacher and practiced by the student. As Hunter advocated, learning is efficient and predictable. The objectives are predetermined by the teacher and fixed, and the content is a set of identifiable skills or quantifiable knowledge. Most often the pedagogical approach includes direct instruction, modeling, and practice. The teacher holds the knowledge and delivers it to the student who practices mastery before being tested on an aligned assessment. The students are expected to apply the knowledge gained from direct instruction first in a guided activity and then independently. Students can and do work together during guided instruction, but independent practice is generally reserved for individual work time.

LESSON PLAN COMPARISON: THE BEHAVIORIST APPROACH TO TEACHING METAPHOR

To illustrate the affordances and limitations of each of our five methods, we offer an example in every chapter on the same topic: teaching metaphor. We recognize that many of our readers are not language arts teachers; we chose this topic because it has many facets that can be prioritized, depending on the method of instruction and aims of the teacher. Also, we are fairly certain that most of you learned about metaphors at some point in your lives, so the topic is accessible.

In the behaviorist approach, remember that the outcome is for students to demonstrate behavioral change within a certain set of conditions. Behaviorism is a potentially useful and efficient way to teach students the definition, identification, and creation of metaphors within the limits of certain parameters. Figure 3.1 provides an example of a behaviorist approach to teaching metaphor that could be appropriate for middle grades.

CRITIQUES AND CONSIDERATIONS

As with all approaches, there are strengths and weaknesses in planning by objectives. Advantages include a sharp focus on what students are to learn. Objectives make sure that directions are clear and transparent and everyone in the class ought to know the expectations. Moreover, this approach makes sure that teachers pay attention to what was supposed to be learned. This approach is not interested in collateral learning—that is, what may have been learned aside from the objectives.

It is important to note that the Hunter model and the behaviorist approach to learning have been widely critiqued (see Ellis & Bond, 2016). Although parts of the learning theory were research-based, as a model that was used almost exclusively after the publication of *A Nation at Risk* (National Commission on Excellence in Education, 1983), it fell short of its promise to singularly increase rigor and performance on standardized testing. While we believe this model has merit for certain aspects of learning, we agree that there are limitations to this approach. First, not everything that is important to learn can be encapsulated in a behavioral objective. If a teacher states that she wants her students to learn to appreciate symphonies, she may be judged vague and wishy-washy by those who prefer strict behavioral-style objectives. Second, behavioral objectives do not allow for flexibility and impromptu lesson changes. Teachers may want to capitalize on a teaching moment—perhaps some political affair seen on TV—but this approach requires adherence to the objectives. In addition, students may learn all sorts of things from any given objective, but in this approach, ideally, one only measures what the objective seeks. If students learn that chemistry is fun, or if they happen to discover something unforeseen in a lab, this matters little to those who stay focused on behavioral objectives. Yet unanticipated learning can fuel motivation and higher-level learning. We will explore such approaches in subsequent chapters.

Figure 3.1. Hunter Lesson Plan: Teaching Metaphor

Teacher Thinking . . .	Students and Teacher Doing . . .
	Lesson Plan Element: Anticipatory Set
How will I get students' attention and focus their learning?	Hold up two objects: a music box and a school photo. Ask students to complete the sentence: "A music box is like a school photo because . . ." Take several answers, affirming all. Then ask them to complete this sentence: "A music box is a school photo because . . ." Affirm answers, even if awkward.
	Objective and Purpose
State the ABCD learning objective (s) and the purpose for learning. How many do I need?	The students will be able to identify statements of metaphor when given choices among other types of comparisons with 85% accuracy. The students will be able to create three metaphors about a single topic (athletics, school, or cooking). Read the objectives written on the board. Then explain that metaphors are useful ways to discuss items and ideas.
	Input/direct instruction
What kind of information must I provide so that students can meet the objective?	Provide the definition of metaphor: a figure of speech that describes an object or an action in a way that isn't literally true but helps explain an idea or make a comparison. A metaphor does not use like or as (using like or as would be a simile). It equates two things to show an idea or to elaborate upon the things being compared. Metaphors are often used in poetry and literature, and they can also be used to enhance expository or persuasive essays.
	Modeling (I Do)
What ways might I show the students the process or skill? What errors and misunderstandings do I anticipate? How might I correct them?	Give several examples of metaphors, perhaps from your current text or popular songs. • Love is a battlefield. • I am titanium. Now give two examples of a simile and one metaphor. Ask student to identify the metaphor: • The car's engine purrs like a cat. • The car is a beast. • The car runs like a dream. Ask students to come up with examples to share and identify as metaphor or simile.

Teacher Thinking . . .	Students and Teacher Doing . . .
	Checking for Understanding
How will I monitor their progress? Will this be informal or formal? Individual or whole group?	Note how well students are able to differentiate between metaphor and simile. Ask students why metaphors are useful in poetry and literary writing (they make ideas interesting; they show characteristics of people or objects, etc.). Ask students to give "fist to five" to show how they feel about their understanding: fist = no clue! 5 = I could teach it!
	Guided Practice (We Do)
What kinds of practice problems might I provide for the skills being taught? How can I organize them so they vary in complexity?	Give students a handout (or write on the board) a series of comparisons. Ask them to identify the metaphors. You may want to also ask them to explain why one or two of them are useful. Ask students to write two metaphors and choose one to write on the board to share.
	Independent Practice (You Do)
What kinds of work should students practice independently toward mastery? Will this be done in class or for homework?	Repeat the guided practice with new metaphors. Have students post their new metaphors on a shared classroom Google document.
	Evaluation and Closure
What should I remind them about that we covered during the lesson? How will I do one last check for understanding?	Ask students to share their definition of a metaphor. Remind them that we identified and wrote metaphors today. On a small sheet of paper, ask students to create one more metaphor as they walk out the door.

Materials: handout with comparisons; quarter sheets of paper

Time and Space: 45 minutes in the classroom

Behaviorist Approach at a Glance

Rationale	Skill Development
Theoretical Background	Teachers can monitor learning through pre-specified behavioral change identified in instructional objectives
Practical Applications	Hunter Model; I Do–We Do–You Do
Learning Aims	Behavioral Objectives: Audience, Behavior, Condition, Degree
Assessment and Evaluation	Aligned and described in behavioral objectives. Must be observable and measurable.
Classroom Interactions	Typically, the teacher is at center stage using direct instruction with guided practice. All students are working on the same content and objective as a whole class.
Critiques and Considerations	May narrow the curriculum opportunities for student exploration and higher-level learning. Does not explicitly respond to the changing learning environment and teachable moments.

Discussion Questions

1. What are the benefits and drawbacks of behaviorist styles of lesson planning and teaching?
2. What kinds of skills and knowledge in your content area are best suited to behaviorism?
3. What kinds of skills and knowledge and understandings are not best suited to behaviorism?
4. What kinds of behaviorist lessons have you experienced? What do you like about them?
5. What are some educational experiences that behaviorist lessons cannot adequately address?

CHAPTER 4

The Constructivist Approach to Lesson Planning

Individualized Meaning-Making

A constructivist approach to learning focuses on the notion that learners individually discover and build their own knowledge (Anderson, Greeno, Reder, & Simon, 2000; Brooks & Brooks, 1999; Gabler & Schroeder, 2003; Waxman, Padrón, & Arnold, 2001). Learners construct meaning by coalescing knowledge they already possess with new information received via experience or reflections (Grennon Brooks, 2004). Proponents of constructivist methods seek to find ways for students to control some of the learning and activities that occur in a classroom; teacher-focused approaches such as lectures are minimized (Moore, 2009). This mode places great emphasis on multiple ways of understanding (Gardner, 1983), multiple forms of representing knowledge (Eisner, 1994), learning rooted in authentic situations (Wiggins & McTighe, 2005), cooperative learning (Moore, 2009), and performance assessments (Marzano, Pickering, & McTighe, 1993).

RATIONALE

Constructivist approaches to lesson planning offer teachers and students the opportunity to make meaning around given concepts and content. Constructivist environments foster students' inquiry, and "questions are recognized as an important window into students' thinking and become the opening for further learning" (Demarest, 2015, p. 10). Learning takes many different forms, and curiosity often leads the way.

THEORETICAL BACKGROUND

Constructivism is both a psychological and philosophical concept. Swiss philosopher Jean Piaget formally introduced the idea of constructivism in

1936 as a "theory of cognitive development explaining how children construct knowledge" (see Conrad, in press). This theory explains how children construct mental models of the world in which they live. Contrary to the dominant notion that intelligence was fixed and that learning occurred when new knowledge was poured into an empty vessel (the brain), Piaget held that cognitive development is a dynamic process where individuals construct knowledge through interactions with their environments. He further added that all children were born with a basic mental makeup upon which new learning took place. In other words, all people have a stored set of knowledge and experiences upon which they make meaning from new information. That information is then organized and stored in *schemas*—a term describing the way knowledge and experience is organized in our brains, often referred to as background knowledge. Rather than learning in a vacuum where new knowledge was added to a blank canvas, Piaget argued that the canvas already has a great deal of information stored on it and when new information is introduced, individuals connect that new information to that which is already on the canvas so as to make sense of it. As such, he argued that everyone makes sense of the world differently.

Jerome Bruner (1960) built on this theory by connecting constructivism to a learning context such as a classroom, framing these ideas through a teaching and learning lens. Drawing on Lev Vygotsky's (1978) work that took Piaget's ideas further to emphasize that constructed knowledge varies across different cultures and environments, Bruner argued that learning is an active process where learners make their own meaning based on their own individual schema, and teachers' role is to create spaces for learners to construct meaning for themselves. Teaching and learning processes built on these ideas shifted from teacher centered to student centered. Bruner suggested the notion of a spiral curriculum where information is organized so that students continue to build upon what they know and have learned over various grade levels. Beyond the spiral curriculum, Bruner's contributions can be found in a number of manifestations within the modern classroom, including the concepts of scaffolding (when teachers provide support to students by incrementally helping them build on their existing knowledge to achieve larger tasks), multi-sensory learning, and curriculum written to accommodate kinesthetic, linguistic, and auditory learners (McLeod, 2019).

Constructivist learning has become a pervasive philosophical approach to teaching, learning, and curriculum writing over the past 50 years. This approach runs contrary to the traditional, teacher-centered, mimetic approach and aims to transform the role of the teacher into a guide or coach who creates spaces for students to grapple with the content so as to make individual meaning. Such an approach increases the likelihood of buy-in from students, increased engagement, and meaningful experiences connected to the content.

PRACTICAL APPLICATION: LESSON PLAN FORMATS

Several constructivist lesson plan models permeate the lesson planning landscape, including the Kodaly method (Boshkoff, 1991); the Moffet and Wagner method (Weiner, 1997); the Science and Technology for Individuals, Societies and the Environment (STISE) method (Park, 1995); the Marzano method (Marzano, Pickering, & Pollock, 2001); the Critical Explorers approach (Duckworth, 2009); and the Universal Design for Learning (UDL) method (Center for Applied Special Technology, 1998). Each of these lesson plan formats places students at the center of learning while casting the teacher in the role of "guide on the side." While teachers may incorporate direct instruction into their lesson plans, the amount of time for such instruction is limited and is not the central focus of the lesson plan. Rather, teachers create spaces for students to grapple with learned knowledge from the lesson in some meaningful, engaging, and purposeful way.

LEARNING AIMS: EMERGENT UNDERSTANDINGS

While behaviorist lesson plans utilize behavioral objectives, constructivist plans emphasize emergent understandings. An *emergent understanding* is a learning aim that focuses on the student rather than the teacher as the central figure in planning and in the day-to-day curriculum. Emergent understandings are still specified and written in ABC format; however, they take into account individual needs by specifying individualized conditions. Again, *conditions* refers to the "C" in the objective, which is the tangible product the students will produce to allow the teacher to assess whether they have learned or not. While the emergent understandings may share the same skill to be learned, how the students illustrate their understanding of that skill may vary. For example, all students may learn to compare and contrast rural neighborhoods with suburban neighborhoods, but some may do so by creating Venn diagrams, some may draw pictures, some may write short constructed responses, and some may create posters. Other times, students may all be drawing a map to illustrate their understanding of the concept being taught. Although the objectives may read similarly, the process of learning, and at times the outcomes, are varied and relate to the specific students in the class.

Emergent understandings are written by the teacher specifically with students' background knowledge in mind; this activates students' schema, or background knowledge. The focus of the understanding is on meaning-making: How will the student put their own stamp on the learning? Emergent understandings need not be the same for the entire class; they may include individualized goals with different yet specific conditions for demonstrating knowledge. Assessments may be internally or externally created, but they should often call for variety in how students display their learning.

While there are many constructivist lesson planning models, we utilize the EEL DR C model to help us illustrate what a constructivist lesson might look like in practice. EEL DR C is an acronym that stands for *enroll, experience, label, demonstrate, review*, and *celebrate*, which are the six elements of the lesson plan. Though other constructivist models such as Eleanor Duckworth's (2009) Critical Explorers may offer more complex forms of planning, the EEL DR C model serves as a good entrée into constructivist lesson planning for those new to this approach. The EEL DR C model, created by DePorter, Reardon, and Singer-Nourie (1999) and based upon the Quantum Learning Model (DePorter & Hernacki, 1992), prescribes a six-step process that focuses on student learning styles, and individual motivation, and multiple intelligences (see Gardner, 1983). EEL DR C lessons aim to increase student engagement by being purposeful about engaging students while making room for as many learning modalities as possible to help students connect new information to their individual schemas. Further, the EEL DR C model encourages teachers to always deliver content that is scaffolded and multisensory, and contains several opportunities for students to process and store information.

Embedded in the EEL DR C model is a sequencing of activities within a lesson that begins with first teaching to the large group, then moving to small groups to strengthen learning, before finishing with individual work that may include answering questions, beginning homework, or taking a test or quiz. The underlying idea behind such an approach is that student risk in the learning process is mitigated by the teacher. The students receive information via whole-group instruction. Then they grapple with the new information in small groups, which lessens risk compared to working in a whole-group format. Finally, they individually illustrate understanding of the concepts covered, which is still somewhat risky but less so because they have already worked with the ideas in small groups and have received peer and teacher feedback (formative assessment).

As mentioned, EEL DR C is an acronym for the six elements of the lesson plan:

1. Enroll
2. Experience
3. Label
4. Demonstrate
5. Review
6. Celebrate

Enroll. Much like the anticipatory set in the Hunter model, *enroll* comes at the beginning of the lesson, lasts no more than 5–10 minutes, and serves as a hook for the students. The enroll should not only create anticipation for what is to come in the lesson, it should serve as a place where students can see why the learning is relevant. The enroll activity is ideally multimodal, where auditory, visual, and kinesthetic learning might take place. Examples of an effective enroll might include storytelling, incorporation of multimedia, role-play, response to questions, a skit, or a pantomime. What is important to note here is that the teacher does not begin the lesson sharing a set of objectives, "I Can" statements, or learning targets before the lesson begins because part of being engrossed in the experience of learning is constructing one's own language around the concepts; stated aims may be shared in the *label* stage.

Experience. Following the enroll element—or sometimes in conjunction with it—teachers create space for students to *experience* content to be learned in that lesson; this serves as an initial exploration of what will be grappled with later in the lesson. The experience should aim to tap into students' natural curiosity, to create engagement for the students, and to allow them to make individual meaning of what is being learned. The experience can take any number of forms, including but not limited to small-group activities, individual activities, games, and simulations. It will be driven by the content being taught, and here teachers can draw on any of the instructional approaches in their pedagogical toolbox to engage students. Varying them frequently would be advisable so as not to create mundane and predictable lessons.

Label. Once the students have had an initial experience, the teacher then *labels* what the students just experienced. For example, a teacher might have students look at a text and underline words or phrases that are repeated, using different ink colors. Once they do that, they are to discuss with a partner what they think each set of repetitions reveals to them about the text. Upon concluding that experience, the teacher labels what they just did as identifying different types of parallelism and doing rhetorical analysis on those parallels. During the label phase, we bring in our whole-group minilessons, teacher demonstrations, and other instructional techniques to provide new information on what has been learned in order to deepen the grappling with content. Teachers can also introduce the emergent understandings for the lesson at this point. The motivating concept for this approach is that we are satisfying the curiosity created through the experience, which, when done well, has led to the students generating questions. Moreover, creating an initial experience before labeling it makes the learning more vivid and memorable. Much as one might be told how to play a game, it is not until one has an experience playing that game that the information on how to play becomes meaningful.

Demonstrate. Once the concept(s) have been labeled and new information has been given, the teacher creates a space for the students to *demonstrate* their learning with a small-group activity. Much like when children are learning to tie their shoes, they may play around with the laces on their own before a parent will explain and show them how to do it. After that information has been received, the child has opportunity to apply the new knowledge by practicing tying shoes. The parent, like a teacher, can offer guidance (conferring) and ongoing feedback (formative assessment). During the demonstrate phase, the teacher confers with the small groups, checks for understanding, asks questions, and pushes students' thinking on the demonstration of learning. Some examples of student demonstration activities include creating videos, co-writing stories or essays, team skits, graphic representations, or creating board games. These demonstrations can also be more traditional, such as collaborating on a handout. The key point is that students show what they have learned in a new and interesting way.

Review. After students demonstrate their learning, teachers create a space for them to *review* the ideas explored so as to strengthen the connections made to schemas, to reinforce their learning, and to provide valuable formative information to the teacher about the needed next lessons. Ideally, review is multimodal, incorporates multiple intelligences, and allows for multiple forms of representing their knowledge in a different context than originally presented in the label or grappled with in the demonstrate sections. Reviews can be as elaborate as students playing review games or teaching what they learned to peers. They can also be as simple as responding to a prompt on an exit ticket, turning to a peer and reviewing learned information, or drawing a learned concept on a piece of paper. The underlying notion of the review section is that practice makes perfect. Extending the shoe-tying example, here children would continue to practice tying shoes on their own.

Celebrate. Finally, teachers conclude with *celebrate*, where they close out the lesson by honoring the students' efforts, successes, and abilities. Celebrate offers teachers the opportunity to build students' confidence and to increase their motivation to learn through celebration of successes, including student effort. Here teachers can also share what is next to come in the unit of study or tie up any loose ends before concluding the lesson. Some examples of celebrations include high fives, team chants, or verbal praise from the teacher or from student to student.

ASSESSMENT AND EVALUATION

Given that the constructivist model of lesson planning holds at its philosophical core the notion that students individually construct knowledge by connecting new information to previously held knowledge (schemas), this model calls for what Eisner (1994) referred to as multiple forms of representation and what the Universal Design for Learning (UDL) dubs multiple means of representation. Students are often evaluated by multiple means of representing their learning with the teacher at times providing choice. One might imagine students being provided a menu of assessment options that include various learning modalities.

To better conceptualize what assessment might look like (in this case a formative assessment), let's consider a sample EEL DR C elementary school lesson on the water cycle. To *enroll* students, I might pull a wet shirt out of a bag and tell them I am upset because my shirt is ruined and I will have to throw it out. The students invariably protest and I ask them why I shouldn't throw out the shirt. Once I get them to elicit that it will dry, I ask where water goes when it dries. After eliciting answers, I place a cloth on each pod of student desks (four desks per pod) and provide each group with a small bottle of water. I ask the students to pour water on the cloths. Then they are directed to measure the diameter of the blotch of water they poured onto the cloth. Each pod will be asked to record in their science journal the diameter of the water and to make a prediction for what will happen to the water in the next 5 minutes.

Then I create an *experience* where the students follow me outside. Each group brings their journals, the cloth, the bottle of water, and the ruler. Once outside (if it is not a warm sunny day, we adapt to use a blow dryer inside), the students lay the cloths down on the ground for a few minutes before measuring for diameter again. The students record their measurements and revisit their predictions. After a few more minutes we repeat the exercise; we continue to repeat until the diameter has lessened a bit.

Once complete, I *label* by asking them what is happening to the water. Eventually, the students verbalize that the water is evaporating; then I point out that this is the water cycle. I explain that much like a wheel, the water cycle goes around and around. Then I offer direct instruction through a multitude of ways, but to offer multimodal instruction, the students watch a short video on the water cycle, with a purpose question to consider (what is the water cycle?). I offer a transcript of the text from the video to differentiate for individual needs. Then students watch a visual presentation to explain the water cycle, writing down new vocabulary on our word wall, including evaporation, precipitation, and condensation. We also examine specific examples of water condensing (ice melting), evaporating (boiling water), and precipitating (pouring out of a watering pot).

The students are then asked to *demonstrate* their understanding; this will be used to formatively assess them. They have several options, or forms of representation, from which to choose to demonstrate their learning. They can draw a diagram, create a multimedia presentation, write a song about the water cycle, or write a short essay. Regardless of what they choose, they must include condensation, evaporation, precipitation, and a clear representation/explanation of the water cycle. Students work in small groups or independently; if they work in groups it will be groups of four.

After 20 minutes or so, students *review* the elements of the water cycle and explain what they did by sharing out what they have created. Having them work in groups allows for more efficient sharing, as it would be time consuming to have them all individually share a representation of understanding. Finally, students respond to the following prompt on an exit ticket (which is used to formatively assess their learning): What is the water cycle? Students again can represent either in writing or in images, but they must include the key words and concepts. Finally, we *celebrate* by making rain with our hands, clapping and snapping to create a summer storm.

Within this example it should be noted that the lesson incorporates myriad intelligences and learning modalities. Students can utilize spatial (drawing diagram), linguistic (recording in journal), interpersonal (working in groups), intrapersonal (exit ticket), bodily-kinesthetic (enroll and experience activity), logical mathematical (measuring diameter), and naturalist (outdoor activity) intelligences. Embedded in this activity are visual, auditory, and kinesthetic learning and students can utilize any number of these intelligences/modalities in their formative assessment. Concurrently, students have their interests piqued by the enroll, are provided an experience to explore, before having the opportunity to apply what they learned through those experiences and the teacher's direct instruction during the label portion of the lesson. The review allows the students to strengthen their the learning while the teacher individually, formatively assesses students.

CLASSROOM INTERACTIONS AND ROLES

The constructivist approach to lesson planning places students at the center of the learning experience with the teacher creating spaces for students to grapple with content for the purpose of individual meaning-making. This approach accounts for different learning modalities (visual, kinesthetic, auditory, etc.) while providing a platform for student understanding of learned content. Pedagogical approaches utilizing this model are varied, including small-group work, individual work, inquiry approaches, and other student-centered methods. Consistent with this method is that teacher-centered, didactic instruction is kept to a minimum with most of lesson time dedicated to students being at the center of the learning. It expresses a belief that those enacting the reading, writing, talking, and doing are the ones doing the thinking. Rather than being a proverbial sage on the stage with all of the knowledge, the teacher serves as a guide on the side providing support to the learners through conferring, questioning, and informal formative assessing.

LESSON PLAN COMPARISON: THE CONSTRUCTIVIST APPROACH TO TEACHING METAPHOR

In the constructivist approach, teachers aim to create spaces for meaning-making. Like behaviorism, constructivism is a potentially useful way to teach students the definition, identification, and creation of metaphors, but unlike behaviorism, constructivism also creates opportunities to apply, analyze, synthesize, and evaluate content. Figure 4.1 is an example of a constructivist lesson plan for teaching metaphor in a high school classroom. Please note that in this lesson, students have already learned to define and identify metaphors. In this lesson, the goal is to analyze metaphors for imagery and what they reveal about the speaker.

CRITIQUES AND CONSIDERATIONS

The constructivist model of lesson planning allows teachers to create moments of curiosity and meaning-making for their students. Through role-playing and other experiences, the students explore big ideas and connections between what could be mundane learning topics. Constructivism in general provides an excellent pathway for motivation, engagement, and personalized meaning around common concepts.

Some critiques of constructivism include that it is too time-consuming and that teacher-centered approaches are more efficient (Anderson, Reder, & Simon, 1999). Others are concerned that believing in subjective understanding can lead to an undermining of any sort of absolute truth (Phillips, 2000). Still others argue that by focusing on depth of content coverage rather than breadth, schools run the risk of producing culturally illiterate students (Hirsch, 1996). Further, at times constructivism may seem to limit learning to the pre-specified understanding. That is, while students have an opportunity to demonstrate learning in a number of ways, they are limited to the concept that has been selected by the teacher. The means are multiple but the ends singular. In future chapters on aesthetic and ecological approaches, we will see ways to facilitate experiences for idiosyncratic, or multiple, outcomes.

Figure 4.1. EEL DR C Lesson Plan: Teaching Metaphor

Teacher Thinking . . .	Students and Teacher Doing . . .
	Lesson Plan Element: Enroll
How will I hook the students to provide an entrée into a deeper experience with the content?	Hand out to the students the lyrics to Justin Timberlake's song "Can't Stop the Feeling." Students follow the lyrics while the song plays. Ask them to listen for and circle on the handout any metaphors they hear.
	Experience
What kind of experience can I create for students to have an initial exploration with the content?	Individually, students create a three-column chart on a piece of paper with the first column reading "metaphor," the second "image created," and the third "what it reveals about the speaker" (the teacher displays a model of this on the SmartBoard or provides a handout or Google doc with the columns already created). Students individually write/enter responses on the chart. The teacher walks around and confers with students to formatively assess, ask clarifying questions, and push students' thinking. To ensure a variety of student responses and to elicit specific metaphors to highlight from the text, as students work, the teacher asks individual students to share one of their responses in the upcoming group activity. Once reconvened, all are invited to share one metaphor, the image created, and what it reveals about the speaker.
	Label
I have to make sure I tell them what they just did. Also, what kind of information must I provide in a minilesson so that students can illustrate understanding of the concept I am teaching? Emergent Understandings: How are we focused on individualized meaning making?	Share, "What you just did is analyze a metaphor. Today we are going to focus on analyzing metaphors in prose to identify imagery and what a metaphor reveals about a speaker." The students will be able to examine how metaphors create images by completing some form of a chart. The students will be able to evaluate what a metaphor reveals about a speaker by responding individually, in pairs, or in small groups to a short, constructed response prompt. Provide a brief minilesson on imagery. Explain what it is and its purpose. Also explain that metaphors not only create images, they reveal things about the speaker. For example, if one writes a number of baseball metaphors, it would reveal that the speaker is likely a fan or player of the game. Check for understanding by asking what questions they have. Hand out an excerpt from Maya Angelou's *I Know Why the Caged Bird Sings*. Before reading the excerpt aloud, ask the students to circle metaphors that they see.

Teacher Thinking . . .	Students and Teacher Doing . . .
	Ask students to share a metaphor they found. On the SmartBoard, using the three-column chart, elicit what images are created and what they might reveal about the speaker.
	Demonstrate
What ways might students illustrate understanding of the concept I am trying to teach? What kinds of spaces can I create for students to grapple with the content?	Give the students a longer excerpt of Ralph Ellison's *Invisible Man.* Tell the students that they are going to identify at least five metaphors. They can use a three-column chart, they might create their own diagram, or they can employ some other form of representing their knowledge. They will do this in small groups (3–5). Tell them that to prepare for an analytical essay, you would like them to write one short constructed response to the following prompt: What images are revealed in Ralph Ellison's *Invisible Man*? What do these images reveal to the reader and what do they reveal about the speaker? They may respond individually, in pairs, or as a group. The teacher walks around the room, checking in with students to formatively assess them and to ask and answer questions.
	Review
How can I formatively assess that students met the learning targets while getting them to capture their thinking?	On an exit ticket, ask students to respond to the following: What is imagery? What can metaphors reveal about a speaker?
	Celebrate
How can I wrap up the lesson and celebrate their learning?	Tell students that we will finish our work next class period (they likely won't finish in time). Go over the emergent understandings with them to reemphasize what they learned today. Remind them that we are building toward being able to analyze various forms of rhetoric for a variety of purposes. Ask students to high-five two students they did not work with today and say, "Metaphors Be With You, Luke."

Materials: iPhone (for iTunes library), "Can't Stop the Feeling" lyrics, *I Know Why the Caged Bird Sings* excerpts, *Invisible Man* excerpts

Time and Space: One class period, classroom with smartboard

Constructivist Approach at a Glance

Rationale	Individualized Meaning-Making
Theoretical Background	Responds to theories of cognitive development as a dynamic process that builds upon prior learning and experience
Practical Applications	EEL DR C, Critical Explorers, Universal Design for Learning
Learning Aims	Emergent Understandings: student-focused aim that fosters individual meaning-making of the content
Assessment and Evaluation	Multiple forms of representation; significant formative assessment to build schemas
Classroom Interactions	Exploration and experience with the opportunity to practice and perform care, interconnectedness, and integrity
Critiques and Considerations	Promotes curiosity and engagement but may be time consuming and may undermine "absolute truth"

Discussion Questions

1. What are the benefits and drawbacks of constructivist styles of lesson planning and teaching?
2. What kinds of skills and knowledge in your content area are best suited to constructivism?
3. What kinds of skills and knowledge and understandings are not best suited to constructivism?
4. What kinds of constructivist lessons have you experienced? What do you like about them?
5. What are some educational experiences that constructivist lessons cannot adequately address?

CHAPTER 5

The Aesthetic Approach to Lesson Planning

Sensory-Rich, Memorable Experiences

Readers may be curious about the concept of aesthetic lesson planning. Aesthetic is a bit awkward to say, let alone spell. But consider for a moment the opposite of aesthetic: anesthetic. We use anesthetics to numb our nerves, to deaden feeling, to put ourselves to sleep. The aesthetic, then, does the opposite—we want our sensibilities fully open, alive, and engaged. This approach to lesson planning is really about being wide awake through and within an educational experience. Grounded in arts-based ideas, aesthetic lesson planning focuses on sensory experiences to guide engagement with content.

What then does it mean to be wide awake? For Maxine Greene, noted philosopher of education, it is the means to the creation of the self. Being fully engaged in experiences, and then reflecting on such experiences, can lead us to a greater awareness of life in general (see Greene, 2001) and greater awareness of content in schools (Uhrmacher, 2009). Many scholars have explored how our senses contribute to the ways we come to know the world (see Arnheim, 1989; Eisner, 1994; Read, 1966). The more we perceive through our senses, the more we come to know. The aesthetic approach to lesson planning places the role of the senses at center stage, utilizing a variety of experiences to create meaning in the content at hand (Uhrmacher, 2009). In contrast to the constructivist and behaviorist approaches, which are more outcome-focused, the aesthetic approach places activities that yield a "wow" experience at the forefront. While outcomes can be, and often are, important to aesthetic lesson plans, meaningful experiences precede them in importance.

RATIONALE

Aesthetic lesson planning can contribute to the engagement and growth of both students and teachers alike. In our research on using the CRISPA approach, which we discuss in depth below, teachers become energized—even "euphoric"—when doing this kind of work (Moroye & Uhrmacher, 2009).

This approach can also help teachers take a subject that they find dull and infuse it with energy and interest for themselves and their students (Conrad, Uhrmacher, & Moroye, 2015). We note that this style of lesson planning, in particular, attempts to stimulate teachers as much as students. Rather than focusing on standards and measurable outcomes, the aesthetic approach invites teachers to focus on the activities they will create for their students, and in doing so, allows teachers to have meaningful experiences themselves. One teacher in particular referred to the aesthetic approach of lesson planning as a "curriculum disruption," or a very different way to go about the lesson planning process from what has been traditionally done (Conrad et al., 2015, p. 9).

Further, our research findings suggest that aesthetic lesson planning enhances creativity by honoring and fostering "lateral thinking" (de Bono, 1970) through making connections among various subject areas and ideas. Our research also indicates that aesthetic lesson planning has the potential to augment episodic memory retention (Uhrmacher, 2009). Distinguished from declarative memory (long-term memory associated with storing and recalling names, dates, and facts), episodic memory is about past personal experiences. We suggest that when educators combine declarative ideas with episodic events, the student has a greater chance of memory retention of both.

Teacher and student growth, joy in learning, creativity, memory retention, engagement with subject matter, and meaning-making can all be accessed through aesthetic experiences, or, as we call them, "wow" experiences. These experiences are characterized by individuals being focused, being present, encountering a feeling of being lost in time, and experiencing full engagement. This chapter is dedicated to helping teachers design and implement such deep experiences for themselves and their students.

THEORETICAL BACKGROUND

The arts (and aesthetics) have a significant history in education, both as a subject of study and as a vehicle for learning other subject areas. We have used four categories to organize this tradition:

1. Discipline-based (art for the betterment of learning art disciplines)
2. Utilitarian (art for non-art ends such as reading or math)
3. Interdisciplinary (art along with other disciplines to study a common theme such as pollution)
4. Transformational (rethinking educational endeavors through artistic and aesthetic viewpoints) (see Uhrmacher & Moroye, 2007)

The aesthetic approach discussed here falls into the transformational category. This perspective allows us to rethink curriculum development—from conception of a lesson, to identifying standards, to the physical creation of the plan, to the reflection on the lesson—through an aesthetic lens that may or may not include the production of art as we generally use that term.

This transformational perspective utilizes the ideas from the pragmatic orientation to thinking about the arts in education (see Uhrmacher, 2009). These ideas are grounded in the works of John Dewey and Elliot Eisner, with our own research extending their theories (see Conrad, Uhrmacher, & Moroye, 2015; Moroye & Uhrmacher, 2010, 2009; Uhrmacher, 2009; Uhrmacher & Bunn, 2011; Uhrmacher, Conrad, & Moroye, 2013).

John Dewey pointed out that the term *aesthetic* derives from the Greek word *aisthetikos,* meaning "capable of sensory perception." In an aesthetic experience, the senses play a dominant role and contribute to the experience having qualities such as enlivened feeling, a heighted sense of perception, and a focus on the moment (see Dewey, 1938). According to Dewey, we may have an aesthetic experience with traditional works of art—painting, dance, theater, music, etc. The arts provide exemplary opportunities for such experiences. But, said Dewey, we can also have aesthetic experiences with any aspect of living. It is not the case that one has a specific type of experience with only certain types of objects or settings and these are called aesthetic. Rather, any experience in any aspect of life has the possibility to become an aesthetic experience. We might drink a cup of coffee and appreciate the warmth of the mug, or the swirling colors of white cream that we pour into the black coffee producing a light or dark brown color. We might also appreciate the rich, earthy aroma. Or we might take a stroll in nature and feel the cool breeze while watching an orange-glow sunset behind rows of trees. And if it is true that we can have aesthetic experiences at home and in nature, then we can also have them in schools.

How might one provide for aesthetic learning experiences in schools? In our earlier work (see Uhrmacher, Conrad, & Moroye, 2013) we referred to this orientation as *perceptual lesson planning*. The *Oxford English Dictionary* defines *perception* as "the process of becoming aware of physical objects, phenomena, etc., through the senses." As this definition suggests, the senses play an important role in planning learning activities. However, we now think that aesthetic is a more encompassing term. *Aesthetic* takes into account becoming aware of entities and qualities through our senses, but also includes having a fully enlivening and engaging experience. The aesthetic approach we focus on in this chapter, which we often simply call CRISPA, includes six dimensions: connections, risk-taking, imagination, sensory experience, perceptivity, and active engagement (see Figure 5.1).

Connections refer to the ways in which people become engaged with the content being taught. We derived these connections partly from the work of Csikszentmihalyi and Robinson (1990) as they studied the aesthetic experiences of art museum officials, and partly from our own observations of artists working with teachers. The connections may be labeled intellectual, sensorial, personal, and social. *Intellectual* connections occur when students connect with the subject matter at hand academically. For whatever reason, some students have an intrinsic interest in a subject area. They connect right away. Other students may get involved by engaging their senses: having them look, touch, smell, or hear (*sensorial* connections). Sometimes a nice pencil or the feel of a glass beaker is enough to spark a connection to the lesson. Still others may relate to the topic by feeling an attachment to the time period (e.g., the Victorian era); culture (the student's culture or their feeling for another culture—culturally responsive pedagogy would fit here); place (some individuals are drawn to particular locations and we note that Indigenous peoples often highlight the importance of place); or through people (e.g., when studying math, one may connect to an understanding of mathematicians). We call these four kinds of attachments *personal* connections. Lastly, we may also find a *social* connection to the class activity. Social refers to the fact that sometimes we become engaged in an activity because of the people around us. Teachers who find ways to connect students to the curriculum in a variety of ways (e.g., small-group work) ensure that they stay engaged throughout the learning experience.

Risk-taking refers to students' opportunities to try something new, to step out of their ordinary routines. Researchers have pointed out that risk-taking may increase students' cognitive development, as well as their creativity, self-motivation, and interest in subject matter (see Uhrmacher & Bunn, 2011). Risk-taking adventures may be high, medium, or low risk; the perception of risk will be dependent upon each student. The teacher must know their students well to orchestrate appropriate risks, but some places to start include preparing students to present an idea in front of the class; helping them share their writing aloud; asking them to work with a new person in class; or suggesting they try out a new form of expression. We do not suggest that risks include activities like cold-calling or other high-pressure endeavors because these may shut down rather than open up learning possibilities for some students. In all cases where risk is involved, the teacher must first create a safe space for learning.

Imagination, in our usage, refers mostly to inward activities of creation. We reserve the word "creative" for outward expressions of one's inward imagination. We also note two types of creativity. The first is where students do something creative for themselves. Writing a haiku for the first time may be creative for students. A second type of creativity is when students create something relatively new for the world. This latter type of creativity is a tall order for K–12 students. In any case, leading to creativity is imagination and here we distinguish four types. Imagination may be intuitive, in which a person has a sudden insight—the lightbulb moment. Imagination may also be fanciful, in which a person combines unexpected elements such as with a dancing tree. Interactive imagination is when a person works with materials for a longer period of time to yield a product. (Writing a poem requires an interaction between the writer and the writing. Once the writing takes shape it places demands on the author and as such there is a back-and-forth activity. Hence our use of the word "mostly" in our definition of imagination above.) Lastly, mimetic imagination is one in which a person mirrors or mimics the creative work of another. These imaginative activities could take the form of role-playing, brainstorming, mixed media projects, or even copying the work of an expert. One colleague, a former English teacher, would have her students copy word for word a paragraph they loved from an accomplished writer. This activity slowed them down, allowed them to feel the words forming in their minds and through their hands, and helped them see the intentional design of punctuation, diction, syntax, and style.

Sensory experience includes at least one person and a sensory interaction with an object or place. The students use their senses to investigate and engage with the object in order to discern its various subtle qualities. Examples in the classroom might include looking at snowflakes under a microscope or sifting grains of sand through a screen to find artifacts. Sensory experience also refers to a sensory-rich environment that enhances the student's experience. Obvious examples include math manipulatives or science experiments, but more subtle sensory experiences might include background music during a writing activity or using drums to play the rhythmic meter in sonnets.

Perceptivity describes a deepened sensory experience during which one thoroughly examines an object using one or more senses. One might think of perceptivity as an elongated sensory experience with the goal of helping students deeply examine a text or object to see or re-see in order to know more. In this case, the senses are used to directly know more about an object, such as a bird's nest. How are the twigs and leaves woven together? Might we distinguish various odors? What do the sounds of the materials teach us? The image of a person standing for a long time before a painting in an art museum might be helpful in thinking about perceptivity. Here the person is taking the time to look for subtleties that distinguish the painting, such as brushstrokes in a particular area of the painting or the shading of an object within the image.

Active engagement requires students to fully participate in their own learning. This includes physical activity, making choices, and creating personal meaning. Teachers may work with students to create a menu for ways to represent their learning, or the class may work through an experiential problem, such as role-play, debate, or simulation. Central to this element is that students are active participants in their own learning.

Figure 5.1. CRISPA Dimensions of Aesthetic Lesson Planning

Dimensions of Aesthetic Lesson Planning	Description
Connections	The ways in which an individual interacts with the subject matter. These connections may be intellectual, sensorial, personal, or social.
Risk-Taking	Students' opportunities to try something new, to step out of their normal realm of experience. Risks are different for different students.
Imagination	The manipulation of ideas and qualities, which may be characterized in several ways: • *Intuitive:* a person has a sudden rush of insight • *Fanciful:* a person combines unexpected elements such as a dancing tree • *Interactive:* a person works with materials in a back-and-forth style to yield a product • *Mimetic:* a person imitates another's creativity
Sensory Experience	Includes at least one person and a sensory interaction with an object. It also refers to a sensory-rich environment, like music playing during a writing activity.
Perceptivity	A deepened sensory experience. Perception is an achievement and as such can be developed. As an example, we could look at almost any object and notice its surface features, but when we really look and examine it, we begin to notice its subtle qualities.
Active Engagement	Students are in the driver's seat. They should be at the helm of their own learning. This could include making sure they are physically active, or intellectually creating meaning, or making choices about how to represent their knowledge.

PRACTICAL APPLICATION: LESSON PLAN FORMATS

A number of endeavors fit under the designation of an aesthetic approach to education. In the 1960s the Central Midwestern Regional Educational Laboratory (CEMREL) created curricula and offered teacher training toward an aesthetic education program. Their aim focused on aesthetics as related to the physical world, art, the creative process, artists, culture, and the environment (Madeja & Onuska, 1977).

The Getty Foundation in the 1980s offered up aesthetics as one component of its orientation to discipline-based art education. In this model, art education focused on aesthetics as a way to understand and explore the intent, value, and appreciation of aesthetic objects. Currently, the Lincoln Center Institute in New York; the Kennedy Center's Changing Education through the Arts located in Washington, D. C.; and Think360Arts in Denver, CO, each explores aesthetics as a way to focus the educational process on qualities such as wide-awakeness, imagination, artistic inquiry, appreciation, and sensory capabilities.

It should also be noted that several types of schools have oriented themselves to put aesthetics at the core of the teaching and learning process. Waldorf, Montessori, and Reggio Emilia schools each weave artistic work into academic disciplines. Finally, Kristen Baxter's (2019) approach to vibrant art lessons serves as another example of aesthetic lesson planning. Baxter's method places student experience at the center by focusing on dialogue, visualization, and demonstration among other teaching strategies.

These aesthetic approaches to lesson planning all share in placing a focus on both the experience of students as well as the teacher in creating the lesson plan. Along with increasing the likelihood that students will buy into and even enjoy the learning, teachers can take pleasure in the act of designing lessons, thereby shifting the traditional paradigm of lesson plans being things done for others (e.g., administrators) to lesson plans being artistic, rewarding endeavors in themselves.

Having indicated a few examples where aesthetics takes center stage in the teaching and learning process, we now return to the exploration of one approach that we call CRISPA. The six elements of an aesthetic experience (CRISPA) can be used in different combinations and for various reasons. Teachers might anticipate their use while planning their lessons, or turn to them in the moment to energize an otherwise bland class session. Regardless of when they are utilized, the elements of CRISPA can be intentional curricular choices that increase the likelihood of students having aesthetic experiences during a lesson. CRISPA itself does not designate the specific order of the lesson, nor are all six elements required for each lesson plan. CRISPA elements are like colors on an artist's palette: available for use when and if they would complement the whole picture. Oftentimes, teachers use the lesson plans required by their schools or districts and then add CRISPA as an overlay to the existing curriculum. We want to stress that one does not need to learn a whole new way of lesson planning in order to use CRISPA. CRISPA can be incorporated in any of the other styles of lesson planning (Uhrmacher et al., 2013). We return to this important idea in the final chapter of the book.

LEARNING AIMS: EXPRESSIVE OBJECTIVES

As we have discussed in each chapter, the learning activity may begin by thinking about the aims for the activity. For a behavioral lesson, this is a behavioral objective; for a constructivist lesson, this is an emergent understanding. For an aesthetic lesson we focus on what Eisner has called expressive objectives (Eisner, 1967), which he later termed "expressive outcomes." Eisner argued that teachers need not begin with behavioral objectives in order to design a meaningful educational experience for students. "One can, and teachers often do, identify activities that seem useful, appropriate, or rich in educational opportunities, and from a consideration of what can be done in class, identify the objectives or possible consequences of using these activities" (quoted in Flinders & Thornton, 2012, p. 113). Further, a pre-specified objective is not adequate to capture all the learning that may occur during a meaningful experience; it narrows the learning. Rather than specify what likely cannot be predicted, Eisner (2005) suggested that we utilize an *expressive* objective, which

> does not specify the behavior the student is to acquire . . . [but instead] describes an educational encounter: it identifies a situation in which children are to work, a problem with which they are to cope, a task in which they are to engage . . . [it] provides both the teacher and the student with an invitation to explore, defer, or focus on issues that are of peculiar interest or import to the inquirer. (p. 34)

Expressive objectives are broad and focus on the experience rather than what the student should be able to do after the activity; the experience itself is most important.

In summary, an expressive objective describes the educational experience or activity. It is brief, open-ended, and leaves plenty of room for the unfolding of a variety of learning outcomes. Here are a few examples that can guide the learning experience:

1. Students will explore the wildlife habitat at the park across from school.
2. The class will examine and appraise the significance of *I Know Why the Caged Bird Sings* by Maya Angelou.
3. The class will visit the nearby retirement home and will read with the residents.
4. Students will design an experiment to understand the water cycle.
5. Students will examine and explore the purposes of 3–5 electronic and print political campaign advertisements.

Below we show an example of a CRISPA lesson. If teachers are going to plan a single lesson with these ideas, we suggest the framework of creating the expressive objective; designing the experience from the inside out; building out the experience by looking at the CRISPA menu; sequencing the events (including a critique of the experience); and adorning the material lesson plan.

As with any lesson plan, a teacher must first decide what they are going to teach. The teacher might consult state standards, a district or school curriculum, or some other scope and sequence guide. Once the teacher has selected what to teach, for example, to understand the role of media in a political campaign, rather than write measurable ABCD objectives based on the topic, the teacher would create an *expressive objective*. The expressive objective, as mentioned previously, is a brief description of the experience the teacher hopes to provide for the students related to the content being taught. For the topic we selected on the role of media in a campaign, we have created the following expressive objective: "Students will examine and explore the purposes of electronic and print political-campaign advertisements." Here we wish to give them an experience interacting with the media specifically related to a political campaign.

Now that the expressive objective is in place as a guide to the lesson, we can begin to design the experience from the inside out. This is where the C of CRISPA elements comes into play. Although the CRISPA elements could be used in any sequence and they don't all have to be used all the time, we recommend starting with connections. We argue that if students don't feel connected to the content or the experience, they are unlikely to engage fully in the lesson. In starting with connections, we attend to the four types: intellectual, social, sensorial, and personal. We ask, "In what ways can we get students to make meaningful connections to the content?"

Students who are interested in politics or media have an intellectual connection. They are already inherently connected in some way to the content because of their prior interest in the topic, and we can leverage that to deepen their engagement. Student buy-in is likely already in place for whatever lesson we create on this topic. To make a social connection, we might have the students work in groups to categorize websites and other sources. Utilizing group learning creates a space for students to connect socially while working through the content, offering opportunity for collaboration, discourse, and personal connection. A sensorial connection could be made by asking students to bring in campaign materials that they have received at their homes. Here we can have students not only make a real-world connection to their lives, but also give them space to engage their senses with the materials they bring in. Finally, creating a personal connection might include the students' researching current and previous candidates, learning about their cultural backgrounds and considering how that background might influence the candidate's perspectives. In just thinking through the category of connection, we can see how the lesson starts to take shape. Even though we don't know what it will look like at the end, we are building from the inside out. As we are brainstorming what this experience would look like, we can think about whether every student needs to bring in campaign material. Might we allow the students to choose what they would prefer to do, a tenet of perceptive teaching? Opportunities abound for differentiation as well. By focusing on the C of connections, we now have a remaining menu of RISPA elements to draw upon.

The next stage is building out the experience by looking at the remainder of the CRISPA menu. As teachers we know the core of the experience will include collecting various forms of media—paper and electronic from local, regional, and international sources—but the question we have to ask ourselves is, "Which elements of CRISPA will make this content come alive in a meaningful way?" In thinking about our lesson, we might decide that we want to focus on creating a sensory experience with the materials. (Note that the sensorial in connections is reserved for the purpose of drawing students into the lesson. The S for sensory experience in CRISPA is for the purpose of greater exploration and fits into the body of the lesson.) We might have them focus on social media ads, radio spots, or print materials and have them describe three kinds of media with all five senses. We could have them record these or share them verbally with their small groups, all the while checking for understanding. We might then go to a deepened sensory experience, also known as perceptivity, by having them focus on one of the five senses for each campaign artifact. We would ask them to spend three minutes per artifact focusing on their observations. They might then share with a partner what their observations tell them about those media forms. This activity in and of itself is a form of risk-taking in that we are asking students to share original impressions based on their experiences rather than answering predetermined questions with right or wrong answers.

To this point, we have focused on sensory experience, perceptivity, and risk-taking. Now we ask ourselves, what else can we do to help students realize the expressive objective? Perhaps we can utilize imagination and active engagement to interpret and evaluate the purposes of these campaign ads. Imagination might help students step into the role of the politician. With a partner, they might take turns acting as if they are one of the politicians in an ad that they have been examining. Here, students are invited to explore the central message of the politician and articulate it using that politician's voice in a role-play. Students will have been prepared to do this effectively because of their perceptivity experience. If time allows, and to further enhance risk-taking, we might invite a few students to share with the entire class. To round out the experience using all CRISPA elements, students can be actively engaged by creating their own campaign advertisements using a format in which they are interested and for an office of their choice, be it president, mayor, city council member, or school treasurer. This last activity can also serve as one of their primary assessments for the lesson or unit. We would like to point out that active engagement was evident throughout the lesson, but we are intentionally increasing it for the assessment.

The next step we may have to take in creating the CRISPA lesson is sequencing the events. It is possible that the teacher has, in the process of brainstorming through the lesson, already sequenced the lesson. However, it is possible that teachers will need to sequence all the great ideas they came up with in some logical manner. We do not prescribe any sequence for using the CRISPA elements in a lesson, but we do suggest that teachers pay attention to the beginning, middle, and ending as they design the complete experience.

Continuing with our example, sequencing the political campaign materials lesson, teachers might begin by having students listen to a short political ad on the radio before doing a pair-share around the question: "How do you think that ad is trying to make you feel?" This warm-up serves as a model and guide to what the students will do in the lesson. Drawing upon the activities created, we might then share our list of resources with the students to help them prepare for identifying and exploring the campaign ads. We would include among the sources they will identify the campaign ad that they brought in from home (if they were able to do so). Giving them a set amount of time to secure at least three campaign artifacts, we could then introduce the sensory experience with each for a minute or two, asking them to record those experiences with one artifact on a piece of paper. Using the one artifact, we could then have them focus on one of their senses to engage in perceptivity for 2 to 4 minutes. We may then have them share those experiences within their group. At this point, we can provide a graphic organizer to help them in interpreting and evaluating the purposes of the campaign ads they selected. Depending on the length of the class period, we will likely have to cut this experience short and either carry it over into the next day or assign what they do not complete for homework. We might also decide to eliminate or carry over the activity where students get into the role of the politician. Here it should become clear that sequencing the experiences is critical from a pacing standpoint. What is particularly valuable is that the CRISPA lesson plan helped the teacher over-plan, which is crucial from a classroom management perspective, while also offering flexibility to make curricular decisions on whether to include all of the experiences created by drawing upon the six elements of CRISPA.

Finally, we can conclude the lesson by considering how we are going to critique the experiences and content coverage from the lesson. We might ask students to reflect on and discuss with their group what it was like to closely examine a political ad. We could also ask (tying back into the expressive objective) what, in their opinion, are the purposes of political ads? Opportunity also exists for the teacher to point to where the students will go next when the class reconvenes. This type of activity gives the students space to capture their thinking and reflect on the content as well as their experiences while allowing the teacher to critique or assess both.

Although not a part of the student experience, we also suggest that teachers adorn the material lesson plan with quotations, colors, and graphics (if they so choose). It is not mandatory, but we believe that teachers who attend to this aspect of the lesson planning process will find the lesson plan engaging when they return to it a year later.

ASSESSMENT AND EVALUATION (CRITIQUE): EVALUATE, ASSESS, REFLECT

For aesthetic lesson planning we recommend the word *critique* to describe the kind of assessment and evaluation that takes place. Critique does not mean saying negative things about one's skills or end products. Rather, in this approach, critique is a way to disclose the important aspects of students' learning. We suggest two main categories of critique: the development of student interests and growth; and their performances in demonstrating what they have learned in particular subject areas. As we noted, a good critique should help students see the ways in which they have grown and the ways in which they can continue to grow; a critique is not an end in itself. The teacher can elicit self-reflection in students by asking what was of interest to them in the activity and what they need or would like to do to extend their learning. A critique may also take the form of a whole-group discussion about a particular student's work and how it affected others. A critique may also focus on how various works speak to each other and extend the learning for all involved. In short, a critique in the form of an evaluation opens up possibilities for future growth.

CLASSROOM INTERACTIONS AND ROLES

In order for aesthetic lessons to work optimally, we offer the following considerations: modeling, classroom culture, dialogue, and opportunity, derived and modified from Nel Noddings's suggestions for teaching caring (1992). First, teachers may note that in order for students to take risks, it is important for teachers to model risk-taking alongside their students. Subsequently, a culture of risk-taking can be built. Once students know that these kinds of activities are utilized and prized, they will be more likely to engage in them. Third, we recommend that teachers have dialogue about the aesthetic orientation. Teachers should explain why they are providing opportunities for aesthetic experiences and what the intended outcomes should be, and they should listen to students' ideas and reflections about those experiences. By providing numerous opportunities for such experiences, students and teachers can become more comfortable taking risks and expanding their willingness to try new things.

LESSON PLAN COMPARISON: THE AESTHETIC APPROACH TO TEACHING METAPHOR

In creating a CRISPA lesson, we first aim at creating the expressive objective. As you see in Figure 5.2, the expressive objective in this case is: students will create metaphor books so they can see that metaphors are all around us. Students will also consider how metaphors help them communicate. An expressive objective does not need to take into account all outcome possibilities, which could be many. The goal of this kind of objective is to focus on an activity that students should find enjoyable and edifying. The next step is designing the experience from the inside out, focusing on connections. In the chart, we see that the four types of connections—intellectual, social, sensorial, and personal—are all present, but, it's not essential to include all four in any individual lesson. The next step in this process is building out the experience by looking at the CRISPA menu. In this phase, the lesson is planned by thinking about risk-taking, imagination, sensory experiences, perceptivity, and active engagement. We remind the reader that our argument is that when these dimensions of an aesthetic experience are tapped, the teacher provides the opportunity for "wow" experiences to happen. Of course, teachers cannot force anyone to have an aesthetic experience, but they can provide the opportunity. Finally, teachers ought to pay attention to sequencing the events, and might also adorn the actual physical lesson plan with aesthetic qualities, such as meaningful quotations, colors, and graphics, though it is not a required component of this approach. We refrain from too much adornment in the example below, and thus include a few quotations. For an example of an aesthetic lesson plan that is more elaborately adorned, see the Beethoven lesson plan at www.crispateaching.org/crispa-lesson-plans.html. Note that the lesson shown in Figure 5.2 is geared toward high school students exploring metaphor in their own and others' writing.

CRITIQUES AND CONSIDERATIONS

The aesthetic approach to lesson planning offers teachers the opportunity to create fun, joy-filled experiences for students that are also engaging and meaningful. Further, the process of creating an aesthetic lesson plan can be a deeply enjoyable and engaging experience for teachers. Rather than focusing on outcomes, this approach centers on creating aesthetic experiences for students through exploration of the academic content. Even if a teacher only occasionally creates an aesthetic lesson plan, every day they can enhance current lessons with elements of CRISPA. Teachers may also wish to adorn any lesson with inspirational quotations, images, and colors. The goal of such adornments is to inspire teachers when they return to these lessons later. The lesson plan should not look like an instruction manual for using a microwave. The lesson should be inspiration and draw the teacher into it immediately.

Some critiques of aesthetic lesson planning come from those who believe that predetermined objectives aligned to a particular outcome is essential to optimal learning. Those espousing to an essentialist philosophy where certain core content should be the focus of education might also be critical of an aesthetic approach. Further, those who believe all educational outcomes must be measurable might be resistant to an aesthetic orientation.

Figure 5.2. CRISPA Lesson Plan: Teaching Metaphor

<table>
<tr><th>Teacher Thinking . . .</th><th>Students and Teacher Doing . . .</th></tr>
<tr><td colspan="2">Lesson Plan Element: Creating the Expressive Objective</td></tr>
<tr><td>What am I going to teach that is in the curriculum?
How can students have a wow experience with the content?</td><td>We will explore the ways in which metaphor influences how we communicate.
Students create metaphor books so they can see that metaphors are all around us.
Students also consider how metaphors help them communicate.
"Books are the mirrors of the soul."
—Virginia Woolf</td></tr>
<tr><td colspan="2">Designing the Experience from the Inside Out: Connections</td></tr>
<tr><td>Looking at the four types of connections, in what ways can I help the students make meaningful connections to the content?
Intellectual: Some students will connect to the ideas right away. My task is to keep them engaged.
Social: Some students will connect to the content through social interactions.
Sensorial: Some students will connect to the content through any or all of their five senses.
Personal: Some students will connect to the content through personal connections to time, culture, place, or people.</td><td>Intellectual Connection: Students who love language and poetry will be engaged.
Social Connection: Students bring an object from home and share with a partner a response to the prompt: This is a (object they brought in). If it wasn't a (blank) it would be . . .
Sensorial Connection: Students go to six different stations to explore various objects. We are using objects so everyone has a concrete connection to the abstract idea of metaphor. They select one item from each station and write an original metaphor in their metaphor book.
Personal Connection: For the objects they select, ask students to consider, "Where have I seen this in my life?"</td></tr>
</table>

Teacher Thinking . . .	Students and Teacher Doing . . .
Building Out the Experience by Looking at the RISPA Menu	
What else can I do to help students realize the expressive objective? Consider risk-taking, imagination, sensory experience, perceptivity, and active engagement.	*Risk-Taking*: Students report out one metaphor they created in their book. This will be risk-taking for many students. *Sensory Experience*: Students will use various senses to explore the objects, and not just rely on its visual appearance. *Imagination*: Students create metaphors and explain how the metaphor is appropriate. Example: How is a lunchbox a battlefield? How is a shuttlecock a representation of freedom? *Active Engagement*: Students take charge of creating their metaphor books with various papers and markers. They create metaphors based upon objects found on thematic tables around the room. *Perceptivity*: Students will choose and closely examine one item from each station. *"Eyes are windows to the soul."*
Sequencing the Events	
How will I open the lesson? (Beginning) What is the order of experiences? (Middle) How will I critique the students' experience? (End)	*Beginning*: Students participate in a warm-up activity to get them thinking about metaphors. They will have brought an object from home to share with a partner by saying to the partner: "This is a [object they brought in]. If it wasn't a [object they brought in] it would be . . ." (*connections & active engagement*). For example, "This is a spatula; if it wasn't a spatula it would be a baseball bat." Then the partner replies with a creative response. In this case: "It could be a lion's tail." *Middle*: Next, students create their metaphor book using several pieces of paper, stapling them together. They create a unique cover with pictures, sketches, and a title (*active engagement* & *imagination*). While they are creating their books, I will give the students a handout with a list of words. The words will suggest concepts that could be related to concrete objects. They will connect objects around the room with abstract concepts to create their metaphors. Concepts on the list will include such words as freedom, strength, perseverance, failure, emptiness, love, redemption, joy, punishment, battle, loneliness, and hope.

(continued)

Figure 5.2. CRISPA Lesson Plan: Teaching Metaphor *(continued)*

Teacher Thinking . . .	Students and Teacher Doing . . .
	Sequencing the Events (continued)
	After creating their books students pair up and go to six stations around the room (*active engagement* & *connections*). Each station has objects that are thematically related. For example, one station may be about food and contain items related to serving or eating food. Another station may be about sports and will contain items such as a shuttlecock or a baseball or a football. At each table students choose one item. They engage their senses to explore the object (*sensory experience*) and then do so more deeply with one sense (*perceptivity*). It could be a lunchbox on the food table. Then, in their metaphor books, students connect the lunchbox to an abstract concept from the list provided or another concept they choose. They write that connection in the form of a simple metaphor. For example, "This lunchbox is a battlefield." Underneath the simple metaphor, students write a brief explanation, such as, "Each item of food is fighting for my stomach's attention" (*imagination and active engagement*). *End*: Students work individually to review their self-created metaphor books and to refine their ideas. I will invite them to sketch images that relate to their metaphors (*imagination* and *active engagement)*. Students then move into small groups to share out at least one metaphor from their books (*risk-taking*). They will discuss in small groups and then as a whole class the effects of using interesting metaphors in communication. Elicit: vivid language, relatable imagery, and new ways to express ideas. Writers use metaphor to make an impact on the reader, to expand concepts, and to create texture and interest. Metaphors help define a writer's style alongside other literary devices. In order to further explore the use of metaphors and the ways in which they influence how we communicate, students will write an extended metaphor based upon one in their metaphor book. *"Do not fear mistakes. There are none." —Miles Davis*

Materials: 8 x 10 sheets of paper, 5 pages per student. Markers, crayons, etc. for drawing on metaphor books. About 5 objects per table for 6 stations (number of tables could be reduced for smaller classroom sizes). Consider objects related to food, sports, TV & movies, books, home maintenance, and sewing.

Time and Space: Classroom space requires tables and/or moving of desks to create stations. Time for activities is 50–60 minutes or more depending on discussion time.

Adornments: Quotations, photos, sketches, and other interesting inspirations

Aesthetic Approach at a Glance

Rationale	Engagement and Growth for Teachers and Students Alike
Theoretical Background	All experiences have the potential to be "wow" experiences, even in classrooms. Teachers can create the conditions for such experiences and therefore foster meaning, memory retention, and creativity.
Practical Applications	CRISPA; *Create* the expressive objective, *Design* the experience from the inside out, *Build* out the experience by looking at the CRISPA menu, and *Sequence* the events. Teacher may wish to also *adorn* the lesson.
Learning Aims	Expressive objectives
Assessment and Evaluation	Productive critique of work created and experiences had
Classroom Interactions	Community of caring learners who take risks
Critiques and Considerations	Designed for meaningful experiences with pre-specified outcomes taking second stage

Discussion Questions

1. What are the benefits and drawbacks of aesthetic styles of lesson planning and teaching?
2. What kinds of skills and knowledge in your content area are best suited to aesthetic lessons?
3. What kinds of skills and knowledge and understandings are not suited to aesthetic lessons?
4. What kinds of aesthetic lessons have you experienced? What do you like about them?
5. What kinds of aesthetic experiences have you had outside of education? What did they mean to you?

CHAPTER 6

The Ecological Approach to Lesson Planning

Real-World Relevance and Connections

Not an environmental science teacher? Don't worry! Keep reading! Ecological lesson planning refers to any type of lesson—not just on "environmental" topics—that includes connections to people, the planet, or local and global communities. "Ecological" by definition describes "interrelationships between living organisms and their environment" ("Ecological," 2019). An environment can include people, objects, conditions, or influences that surround a living thing. An *ecological* lesson breaks down the barriers between school and life, between content and communities, focusing on both experience and exploration. All subject areas—math, science, art, language arts, social studies, PE/health, music, world languages, and vocational studies—hold multiple possibilities for such connections. While environmental topics may certainly be explored in this way, so can others. In this chapter we provide two ways of thinking about ecological lesson planning: *place-based curriculum design* and *ecological mindedness* (henceforth referred to as *ecomindedness*).

Place-based curriculum design (PB) begins where you are. In other words, the local context and community provide inspiration for what, how, and where to teach. "Place-based education might be characterized as the pedagogy of community, the reintegration of the individual into her home ground and the restoration of the essential links between a person and her place" (Lane-Zucker, 2004, p. ii). Teachers and students who use a place-based approach might begin with the simple (and complex) questions: "Where are we?" and "Who lives here?" Such questions lead to local investigations that span geography, science, social studies, mathematics, language arts, literature, and the arts. In addition to providing context for the curriculum, place-based lesson planning includes an action component. Once teachers and students explore their communities, they respond in various practical ways, from connecting with elders to cleaning a local pond to writing politicians regarding important issues.

Where place-based curriculum design focuses on local investigations, the themes of ecomindedness center on care, interconnectedness, and integrity, which are "characteristics of the experience as well as sensibilities, or habits of mind, developed by those engaged in the experiences" (McConnell Moroye & Ingman, 2018, p. 1128). Teachers may build learning experiences explicitly around these themes, or they may infuse the themes into a lesson they have already written in order to enhance relevance for the students and to guide an exploration of the relationship between humans and their communities. Our research indicates that teachers are easily able to incorporate the themes in their current work and that they are compatible with required standards while increasing relevance for students (McConnell Moroye & Ingman, 2018).

RATIONALE

The ecological approach to lesson planning focuses on experience and exploration with attention to the sociocultural context, offering teachers and students a number of potential benefits. The PB component of an ecological approach engages students as "researchers, meaning-makers, and problem solvers" (Demarest, 2015, p. 1). Teachers who are interested and skilled in helping students conduct local investigations "offer young people a vibrant context for traditional knowledge and skills, as well as enduring lessons about how to live their lives peacefully and productively in communities" (Demarest, 2015, p. 2). Ecomindedness has shown to be "relevant for schools in terms of content, engagement, and students' lives; as compatible with standards and other external mandates; and as a form of character education" (McConnell Moroye & Ingman, 2018, p. 1128). Whether teachers undertake a large-scale curriculum reform project through place-based curriculum design, or a daily reinvention of a current lesson plan, the ecological approach can enliven student learning and deepen connections between the human and other-than-human worlds.

THEORETICAL BACKGROUND

When people hear the term "ecological education," they often think first of *environmental* education, but there are distinctions and differences. Originally described by the World Conservation Union in 1970, the general aim of environmental education is to "develop skills and attitudes necessary to understand and appreciate the inter-relatedness among man, his culture, and his biophysical surroundings" (Palmer, 1998, p. 7). Environmental education has had many identities and iterations in the decades since its formalized definition, and may be thought of as education in, about, for (Tilbury, 1995) and with (Moroye, 2010) the environment. Additional perspectives of environmental education include ecojustice education (Martusewicz, 2005), education for sustainability (Sterling, 2001), and others including the two discussed here: place-based curriculum design (Demarest, 2015; Smith, 2007) and ecomindedness (McConnell Moroye & Ingman, 2018; Moroye & Ingman, 2013). Although the iterations of environmental education emphasize different priorities and approaches, all in some way seek to reconnect humans with their surroundings toward the aim of ecological health—including human health and access to clean air and water. Many iterations of environmental education, including the two discussed here, avoid using fear or shame to encourage students to care for the environment. They also resisted issue-based curriculums that isolate specific environmental problems such as pollution, climate change, or biodiversity loss. Some studies have suggested that such approaches can lead to ecophobia (Sobel, 1996) and may not be productive in supporting students' connections to and care for the planet. While environmental issues and problems have their developmentally appropriate place in the curriculum, the ecological approach described in this chapter is intended to be both good for the environment and good for education in that students focus on local places, caring, and connections.

Thus, place-based curriculum design prioritizes exploration and connection to place, to "the ties that connect a person with nature and culture" (Lane-Zucker, 2004, p. ii). PB is often focused on nature and natural spaces, but it may also include investigations of the schoolyard, the neighborhood, and local parks. Such investigations have the potential to revitalize civic life (Lane-Zucker, 2004) and to provide ways for students to deepen their relationships with their human and other-than-human communities. The community becomes a framework for learning about self toward the aim of caring for self and others.

Ecomindedness describes a set of research-based characteristics and habits of mind that may be incorporated into any curriculum regardless of subject matter or grade level. The themes support "green" perspectives in the sense that they draw our attention toward the ways in which we relate to the world and all of its inhabitants. These themes also lead to educative experiences in that they support relevance and motivation to learn more. Ecomindedness themes describe qualities of a student's experience as well as habits of mind they develop.

THEMES OF ECOMINDEDNESS

Care: Care for self; care for animals, plants, and the earth; care for strangers and distant others

Interconnectedness: Acknowledgment of the eclectic and diverse relationships among all things; juxtaposition (seeing and analyzing the placement or physical relationship between things to show contrast and comparison)

Integrity: To act in accordance with one's beliefs; wholeness

ECOMINDEDNESS AND PLACE-BASED CURRICULUM TOGETHER

While they may be used separately, together the local contexts of place-based curriculum intertwined with the global themes of ecomindedness—care, interconnectedness, and integrity—create pathways for exploring nearby communities with an eye toward imagining our global relationships. Place-based curriculum design begins with local investigations: Where are we? Who lives here? How am I connected? Ecomindedness infuses themes of caring for self and others; interconnectedness among all things; and integrity to act upon one's developing beliefs. Therefore, this connection of PB and ecomindedness is a call to engage and explore through direct experience while developing sensibilities that lead to sustainable ways of being and living.

The research on place-based curriculum design (Demarest, 2015) and on ecomindedness (McConnell Moroye & Ingman, 2018; Moroye & Ingman, 2013) indicates that the blending of the two makes curriculum and schooling more immediately relevant and engaging for students. In addition to learning content called for by standards, students learn to ask how they are connected to the local community, including the people, places, and natural landscapes in which they live. This approach inherently increases for the students the relevance of the content being covered. Students explore what they care about and how their own local places are connected to other systems and societies. Further, students ask themselves how they will act upon their developing beliefs. Students see themselves and their own lives in their learning while having choice and input into how and what they learn. Ecomindedness encourages questions about the juxtaposition of parts and wholes, of opposites and contrasts. Juxtaposition allows us to see objects in relationship in physical spaces—the trash can next to the tree; the row of stores alongside a creek—and to notice how they are interacting with each other and what the relationship tells us about humans and their environments. Ecomindedness encourages students to make connections between the self and the community, and the self and the content. In short, place-based lesson planning involves the local contexts; ecomindedness refers to themes that can be included in any lesson, anywhere.

When writing an ecological lesson plan, a teacher may draw upon both or just one of the two components of the model. Place-based curriculum design is a larger undertaking but ecomindedness can easily be used to build any lesson. In the examples that follow, we will apply both place-based curriculum design as well as themes of ecomindedness in the lessons.

PRACTICAL APPLICATION: LESSON PLAN FORMATS

Where behaviorist lessons begin with objectives, constructivist plans begin with understandings to be explored, and CRISPA lessons begin with the expressive objective in mind, ecological lesson plans begin with a particular experience of connection and relationship in mind. Specifically, place-based lesson plans begin with an exploration of where you are—your local community. Ecomindedness lessons begin with asking how we are, or might become, connected to the content to be learned, including where the concepts in the lesson can be localized and discussed.

LEARNING AIMS: EXPERIENCE-BASED OBJECTIVES (EBO)

In this text we have identified a particular objective for each curriculum design focus. Objectives are not neutral; they prescribe and guide a particular type of learning and experience. As Ingman and McConnell Moroye (2019) have argued, experience is inextricably tied to education:

> This underlying definitional relationship—that education is curriculum and curriculum is experience—is not trivial. It reminds us of an important point for educators today: A focus on the experience of students is of primary importance in consideration of their education. (pp. 348–349)

While it may seem obvious that education could only exist through experience, what is not obvious is the central role of planning for experience. In other words, the focus of an instructional objective is typically on the knowledge or skill to be gained, not the experience through which such ideas are explored. To call greater attention to such experiences, Ingman and McConnell Moroye describe what they call *experience-based objectives* (EBO). These learning aims place experience at the heart of the learning; the context and interactions of the educational situation are as important as the learning outcomes. Experience-based objectives, while similar, are different from expressive objectives in that they go further to describe the experience for students, and they always describe the sociocultural context for learning—where and with whom the experience takes place. Both experience-based objectives and expressive objectives focus on experience, but an experience-based objective attends to sociocultural context—place, people, and community—whereas an expressive objective does not.

Such attention to experience has the potential to transform the learning as well as the communities in which such learning occurs. One example described by Taliaferro Baszile (2017) traces the roots of a place-based school whose founders believed that "transformation in education and transformation in society had to go hand-in-hand" (p. 214). Toward that end, the school engaged the local community in a variety of educational experiences that led to "transformative change toward more just futures" (p. 214). We believe that the ecological approach, when designed with experience at the heart of the lesson, has the potential to transform individuals, communities, and our global environmental conditions.

How are EBOs created? An experience-based objective is a teacher and student co-created objective focused on student experience that is flexible and adaptable to different experiences while being responsive to the concepts and skills required by the content. Within this single definition, there are four components to an EBO:

1. Focus on the experience rather than the outcome. Even in the evaluation and assessment, students will be having an experience that enriches their understanding of the ideas. *What* concepts and skills will be explored? *How* will we design the experience to explore them?
2. Involve students in creating the objective. This may be done in advance or during the lesson by giving choices. This aspect of the objective should attend to the personal, cultural, and social contexts of the lesson. *Who* will support students in their learning? *Where* and *when* will students engage with the content? Incorporate adaptable activities to support student interests.
3. Describe and elicit from students the reasons for studying the concept. *Why* is this important? *How* does it connect to students' lives and promote future learning? What other content areas, learning experiences, and skill sets will emerge as significant after this lesson?
4. *How* will students demonstrate their understandings and developing beliefs? The EBO should promote a multiplicity of outcomes. While the core concept may be the same (e.g., finding the area of a rectangle), the students may create floor plans or comic strips or planned animal habitats to show what they know.

The EBO must aim toward an educative experience that connects to students' lives and balances the desires of the student (choice) within the content to be learned. Further, the environment—the classroom culture, systems, physical space, community relations, and other aspects of the context—are expressly included; an EBO always exists in a particular place with particular people, and with attention to students' cultural backgrounds in mind. According to Ingman and McConnell Moroye (2019):

> This criterion is also consistent with practices of culturally responsive teaching by embracing and celebrating student backgrounds, which can be "culturally validating and affirming" (Gay, 2000, p. 29) for students. Further, in requiring

> attention to (and promoting congruence between) school and family life, this criterion aligns with Nieto's (1999) argument that "using the experiences and skills of all families to encourage student learning is a more hopeful and productive way of approaching families than is the viewpoint that students have only deficits that must be repaired." (p. 93)

As you will see in the examples below, an experience-based objective often reads like a brief narrative or description of the experience. There is no prescription as there is with behavioral objectives (the ABCD method), but rather a framework that includes the who, what, where, how, and why of the experience.

LESSON PLAN EXAMPLES

To help more clearly illustrate place-based lesson planning and planning with and for ecomindedness, we offer:

1. An ecomindedness lesson plan template with questions to prompt teacher thinking (Figure 6.2)
2. A sample ecomindedness lesson (Figure 6.3)
3. A place-based lesson plan template that also incorporates the ecomindedness themes (Figure 6.4)
4. A sample place-based lesson using the ecomindedness themes (Figure 6.5)

We share two lesson plan templates to help you think through and plan using the ecological approach. Both templates include in the "Teacher and Students doing . . ." column a list of questions to help teachers orient themselves to this method.

Ecomindedness Lesson

Although ecomindedness themes may be infused into any lesson, they may also be used to design an ecological lesson from the start. While place-based design begins with a local investigation, an ecomindedness design begins by locating the curriculum concept wherever it may exist, near or far. Where can we find commas? Where did the Civil War take place? Where do we see examples of restorative justice? Where are migrating birds going? In what areas and professions do people need to know how to navigate bodies of water? Locating the concept helps students understand the interconnectedness of people, places, ideas, and skills. After locating the concept, skill, or idea, students learn about it through an engaging experience that fosters a sense of care for self and others. Finally, students are invited to live the idea—to think about how exploring the concept helped shape their beliefs and how they might act on them with integrity.

Like PB, planning with ecomindedness also begins with an experience-based objective describing who, what, when, where, why, and how the experience will take place. The experience in an ecomindedness lesson is built from the three themes of interconnectedness, care, and integrity. We can think about the structure of an ecominded lesson plan as having four elements:

- Describe It (Experience-Based Objective)
- Locate It
- Learn It
- Live It

If I wanted to teach the area of a rectangle to my 3rd-grade students, I might start by thinking about the specific standards and concepts I want students to explore. For this example, I am using the Colorado State Standards (see Figure 6.3). Once I have identified my specific content goal, I can begin to design the experience and describe it through the lens of the experience-based objective: "The students learn to see that rectangles can be seen in their immediate environment, including buildings, materials, and even as a way of seeing animals and other objects. They create imaginative representations of animals, explore the kinds of habitat they live in, and compare their own habitats with that of the animals they are creating."

Who: Students with the help of a parent, sibling, or friend.
What: Learn to find area of rectangle; compare areas; consider how much area we need in our habitats.
When and Where: In class and at home after the lesson.
How: Using note cards, blank paper, rulers, measuring tape, and the formula for area, students will explore and compare areas of rectangles.
Why: To learn how finding areas can help us understand how much habitat we each need and how we might ensure all beings have enough space to thrive.

Now that I have described the experience, I will think about how we can begin to find the concept in our immediate lives—where can we *locate it*? I ask students to list on a rectangular note card all the places they see rectangles. I encourage them to see the shapes literally in bricks, sidewalks, barns, papers, and the like, as well as more figuratively as in the general shape of a dog's torso or the long nose of a sloth. In this way, students can see how the world is made up of many shapes that can be identified, measured, and compared.

Figure 6.2. Ecomindedness Lesson Plan Template

Teacher Thinking . . .	Students and Teacher Doing . . .
Lesson Plan Element: Describe It (EBO)	
How can I describe the students' experience? Who, What, When, Where, Why, and How? What standards or curriculum concepts do I need and want to address?	Students have choices throughout their learning experiences.
Locate It	
How can I help students find the content in its "natural" context? Where does this skill, idea, concept, or element of content reside? What examples can they find in their own lives, with their families, and their communities? *Interconnectedness*: Acknowledgment of the eclectic and complex relationships among all things; juxtaposition. How am I connected to the concepts and ideas? How is the content I am studying related to other concepts?	Students may go on scavenger hunts for ideas or skills (where do we find commas? What is the largest image of a bird you can find? Where was the Pythagorean theorem discovered?) by examining materials, various media sources, their own lives and families, etc.
Learn It	
How can I design an experience to help students explore and experience the concept where it is found? In what ways can I help students care about themselves, others near and far, human and non-human? How can I help students understand the usefulness and meaning of this concept for their lives? *Care*: Care for self; care for animals, plants and the earth; care for family, neighbors, and strangers and distant others What does it mean to care about myself? How does caring for myself allow me to care for others? In what ways might I care for others near and far, human and non-human?	The experience may take many forms, but students practice and examine ways that they can learn the content through and with caring about themselves and others. For example, in a study of the playground, students may explore how to care for and feed local and migrating birds and other animals.

Teacher Thinking . . .	Students and Teacher Doing . . .
Live It	
How can I help students think about their learning as a part of their construction of beliefs and values, along with decisionmaking? What values and beliefs are embedded in the lesson? How can I help students develop and act upon those values and beliefs? While some lessons may focus on immediate action, others may introduce a concept and generate many possibilities for living the ideas. For example, students might be introduced to thinking about habitat conservation, but the focus of the lesson is to help them connect their own habitat with animal habitats. *Integrity*: To act in accordance with one's beliefs; wholeness How do I understand and develop my own beliefs and values related to content? What actions can I take, large and small, to act on my beliefs?	Students try out ways of demonstrating their learning and the beliefs they have developed throughout the lesson. This may look different for different students, and idiosyncratic demonstrations and understandings are encouraged and fostered.

Notes:
Materials:
Time and Place:

Next we *learn it*. How can I design an experience that is engaging, informational, and fosters many outcomes? I have students select any animal they want—one that they have seen in the neighborhood or in a book or in a video—and draw it using just rectangles. This requires some imagination, but students have a chance to think about different sizes and relationships among rectangles. To reinforce this comparison, I hand out some colored pencils and have students color their largest rectangle one color and their smallest rectangle another color. Because these drawings are quite fun and interesting, I want them to name their animals and share with each other and to discuss how they know one rectangle is bigger than the other. I help them see that the lengths and widths are longer on the larger shape.

Next, I want them to begin to see how parts of their own lives are made up of rectangles. Using their imaginations and memories, they draw their own room at home, or another room they select. I have them include a few rectangular objects like their bed, dresser, or rug. At this point I want them to not only see relationships among various sizes of rectangles, but also how to calculate how much space they take up and to learn the formula for area. I write the formula on the board and do a few simple calculations with them. Then, I ask them to use rulers to measure the drawings of their rooms in centimeters, then practice finding the area. If their animal drawings allow, they may also calculate the areas of the various rectangles that comprise their bodies.

In order to foster care for themselves and for animals, I want them to think about and compare their habitats. I ask students to draw the habitat for the animal they made, asking what kinds of things go into its space. They can include food, where they sleep, other animals in the family, and other elements they think their animal might need. I ask them to compare their own habitat with that of the animals so they can start to compare and contrast what we all need to live (juxtaposition).

While it may seem strange to ask students to act with integrity related to finding the area of a rectangle, I want them to see that they can use their understanding of area to ask questions and to make judgments about use of space and the necessity of human and animal habitat. I want them to discuss why different animals and different humans need different amounts of space to live. So, for their evaluation, I ask students to go home and measure their room or another space in the house with the help of a family member or friend. This ensures some engagement with others and will extend the learning beyond the classroom. I also ask them to measure the lengths and widths of their bed and one other rectangular object and then calculate the area of each. This gives them practice with the key skill of finding area of a rectangle.

But I don't want to stop there. I ask students to research the animal they drew. They can work with a family member to explore the Internet, books, or other sources to find out more about that animal's habitat. What kind of "room" (den, nest, burrow, hive) does it live in? How much space does it need to live? How many other family members does it live with? What kind of climate is best? Then I ask students to share what they learned about their animal with the class. After our sharing, we talk as a group about how finding the area of rectangles can help us understand what we all need to live. We then discuss how we can be sure we all have space to live. For the culminating project, students talk to a family member or friend about their ideas and understandings about habitat, finding the areas of a rectangle, and making space for all. I invite them to represent their understandings in a paragraph, comic strip, drawing, poem, or other representation they suggest. This lesson can also lead to a discussion in science about habitat, conservation, climate, and the ways different animals depend on each other.

Figure 6.3. Ecomindedness Lesson Plan: Finding the Area of a Rectangle and Comparing Areas of Habitats

Teacher Thinking . . .	Students and Teacher Doing . . .
Lesson Plan Element: Describe It (EBO)	
How can I describe the students' experience? Who, What, When, Where, Why, and How? What standards or curriculum concepts do I need and want to address?	The students learn to see that rectangles can be seen in their immediate environment, including buildings, materials, and even as a way of seeing animals and other objects. They create imaginative representations of animals, explore the kinds of habitat they live in, and compare their own habitats with that of the animals they are creating. *Who*: Students with the help of a parent, sibling, or friend *What*: Learn to find area of rectangle; compare areas; consider how much area we need in our habitats *When and where*: In class and at home after the lesson *How*: Using note cards, blank paper, rulers, measuring tape, and the formula for area, students explore and compare areas of rectangles *Why*: To learn how finding areas can help us understand how much habitat we each need and how we might ensure all beings have enough room *Standard/Curriculum concept:* Colorado State 3rd-Grade Expectation: Measurement & Data: Geometric measurement: Recognize perimeter as an attribute of plane figures and distinguish between linear and area measures. *Colorado Essential Skills and Mathematical Practices:* 1. Make sense of the relationship between area and perimeter by calculating both for rectangles of varying sizes and dimensions. (MP1) 2. Model perimeters of objects in the world with polygons and the sum of their side lengths. (MP4)

(continued)

Figure 6.3. Ecomindedness Lesson Plan: Finding the Area of a Rectangle and Comparing Areas of Habitats *(continued)*

Teacher Thinking . . .	Students and Teacher Doing . . .
	Locate It
How can I help students find the content in its "natural" context? Where does this skill, idea, concept, or element of content reside? What examples can they find in their own lives, with their families, and their communities? *Interconnectedness*: Acknowledgment of the eclectic and complex relationships among all things; juxtaposition How am I connected to the concepts and ideas? How is the content I am studying related to other concepts?	Hand out a 4×6 note card to each student at the beginning of the lesson. Write on the board and ask, "Where do we see squares and rectangles? On the side of your card with lines, list as many places as you can that you see squares and rectangles." Elicit walls and floors, sidewalks, bricks, and more abstract ideas like the body of a lion and the lines between stars in constellations. If there is time, have students walk down the hall to find rectangles.
	Learn It
How can I design an experience to help students explore and experience the concept where it is found? In what ways can I help students care about themselves, others near and far, human and non-human? How can I help students understand the usefulness and meaning of this concept for their lives? *Care*: Care for self; care for animals, plants and the earth; care for family, neighbors, and strangers and distant others What does it mean to care about myself? How does caring for myself allow me to care for others? In what ways might I care for others near and far, human and non-human?	"On the back of the note card where there are no lines, draw any animal you like by just using squares and rectangles. Let's see how fun your animals can look!" Choose one color to fill in your largest rectangle on your animal. Choose another color to fill in your smallest rectangle. How much bigger is your large rectangle? How do you know? Discuss that the lengths and widths are longer. Give your animal a name, decide where it lives, and share that with the person next to you. Hand out a larger piece of blank white paper. "Now think about your own room. Draw the perimeter of your room and any other rectangles you find in there, such as your bed, your rug, etc." Circulate as students draw their rooms and point out the different sizes of rugs, beds, dressers, etc. Now that you have seen that rectangles are all around us, let's figure out how to find out the area, or how big each rectangle is. Give the formula for finding the area of a rectangle: Length x width.

Teacher Thinking . . .	Students and Teacher Doing . . .
	Learn It (continued)
	What is the area of the note card? What is the area of the paper? Now using your rulers, measure the rectangles in your room. How big did you make your bed? Your other objects? Label them on the page (okay to round up). Now take another piece of paper. Draw the habitat for the animal you made. What kinds of things go in its space?
	Live It
How can I help students think about their learning as a part of their construction of beliefs and values, along with decisionmaking? What values and beliefs are embedded in the lesson? How can I help students develop and act upon those values and beliefs? While some lessons may focus on immediate action, others may introduce a concept and generate many possibilities for living the ideas. For example, students might be introduced to thinking about habitat conservation, but the focus of the lesson is to help them connect their own habitat with animal habitats. *Integrity*: To act in accordance with one's beliefs; wholeness How do I understand and develop my own beliefs and values related to content? What actions can I take, large and small, to act on my beliefs?	How much area does your animal need for its habitat? How much area do you need for your habitat? Why do different animals and humans need different amounts of space to live? Elicit size of the animal, number of animals living together, available space, and other creative responses. Evaluation: Go home and measure your room or another space in the house with the help of a family member or friend. Measure the lengths and widths of your bed and one other rectangular object. Calculate the area of each. Research the animal you drew. What kind of "room" (den, nest, burrow, hive) does it live in? How much space does it need to live? What kind of climate is best? How many other family members does it live with? Share what you learn about your animal with the class. How does finding the area of rectangles help us understand what we all need to live? How can we be sure we all have space to live? Talk to a family member or friend about your ideas. Represent your understanding in a paragraph, comic strip, drawing, poem, or other representation.

Materials: Notecards, blank paper, rulers, measuring tape, colored pencils

Time and Place: Cassroom and at home

Place-Based Lesson

A place-based lesson can start with a simple question with complex answers. Asking students, "Where are we?" allows them to imagine the various places they inhabit—their homes; their communities; their schoolyard; their local parks and ponds. Asking them, "Who lives here?" encourages them to imagine their own families, their neighbors, the shop owners; the birds, the reptiles, the insects, the mammals. These are big questions and explorations, and we don't need to tackle them all at once. But selecting a guiding question for investigation is the first step to designing the lesson. Then that investigation can be planned through a digestible lesson that has a series of elements. These are listed below and then incorporated with teacher prompts in the place-based lesson plan template.

Elements of a place-based lesson (see Figure 6.4):

1. Investigative question designed collaboratively with students that honor their past and present experiences
2. Experience-Based Objective
3. Opportunities for direct exploration of places and development of a sense of place
4. (Optional) Exploration of ecomindedness, including caring, interconnectedness, and integrity
5. A way forward through positive action, large or small, through a sense of personal agency
6. (Optional) Interdisciplinary elements.

ASSESSMENT AND EVALUATION

Before moving into our metaphor lesson plan, we want to note that assessment and evaluation in the ecological approach can take on a different character than in other methods. The emphasis in the ecological approach is an experience of content that includes some action component. Assessments, therefore, may include traditional tests and quizzes if appropriate, but should also evaluate student experience and growth, or change in beliefs and calls to action. An exploration of the local park might yield a variety of outcomes for students, including learning the names of plants and animals and the interdependent relationships among them, and also taking action to protect or educate others about the local park residents. Therefore, assessments can and should be both knowledge- and experience based.

Figure 6.4. Place-Based Lesson Template

Teacher Thinking . . .	Students and Teacher Doing . . .
Lesson Plan Element: Investigative Questions	
How might I design experiences collaboratively with students that honor their past and present experiences? Some examples: Where are we? Who lives here? How did our community form? Where does our food come from? Where do we get our drinking water? What migration patterns exist in our communities?	Share ideas and wonderings about their experiences in their communities and how they might explore them.
Experience-Based Objective	
What are the who, what, when, where, how, and why of the experience? Focus on the experience rather than the outcome. *What* concepts and skills will be explored? *How* will we design the experience to explore them? Involve students in creating the objective and attend to the personal, cultural, and social contexts of the lesson. *Who* will support students in their learning? *Where* and *when* will students engage with the content? Incorporate adaptable activities to support student interests. Describe and elicit from students the reasons for studying the concept. *Why* is this important? *How* does it connect to students' lives and promote future learning? What other content areas, learning experiences, and skill sets will emerge as significant after this lesson? How will students demonstrate their understandings and developing beliefs through a multiplicity of outcomes?	Brainstorm responses and possible explorations based upon the investigations. What is important and relevant to study? What kinds of field trips do we want to do? Who are we as individuals and as a community, and how do our cultural and individual experiences support our learning? Discuss reasons for exploring certain places and contexts and how students are connected. What ways can students show what they have learned? Think about maps, brochures, letters, floor plans, or other forms of representation of learning.
Direct Exploration of Places and Development of a Sense of Place	
What opportunities exist for students to explore?	Consider local parks, ponds, open fields, schoolyards, community blocks, local businesses, backyards, government facilities.

(continued)

Figure 6.4. Place-Based Lesson Template *(continued)*

Teacher Thinking . . .	Students and Teacher Doing . . .
Multiple Pathways to Experience and Explore Ecomindedness (Optional for Place-Based)	
What are the pathways to experience and explore caring, interconnectedness, and integrity?	Engage in experiences characterized by care, interconnectedness, and integrity while practicing each as a habit of mind. Care: for self and others near and far (reading to elders; raising money for a boardwalk; raking leaves for the community) Interconnectedness: understanding of relationships (mapping, sources of local products, origins of school supplies, local storytellers) Integrity: acting in accordance with one's beliefs (volunteering at an animal shelter, writing poetry of place to share with others, providing lead-testing kits to community members)
Positive Action	
How can the students act to improve the situation being explored?	Share acts of integrity and collectively plan for further action, exploration, and extensions of learning.
Inter- or Multidisciplinary Explorations	
How might I bring in interdisciplinary learning? Sample interdisciplinary investigations: Has this park always looked like this? Who used to live here before the park was built? What kinds of practices are used to maintain the park? Are they sustainable? How am I connected to this place? What memories do I have of it? What do I want it to be like in 10 years? 20? 200?	Science: Test the water at the pond; collect and classify insects Math: Graph the occurrence of found creatures and objects; create a budget for park improvements Social studies: Create accurate maps; explore the role of a park in a community; explore social inequalities and opportunities; interview those who designed or who care for the park Language Arts: Using all five senses, write poetry about the place; research the history of the park and write an historical account of the humans and animals that have lived nearby; write letters to government officials to request attention or funding for aspects of the park

Teacher Thinking . . .	Students and Teacher Doing . . .
Sample interdisciplinary EBO: Students explore the park through memory and then with a fieldtrip. They map what they remember and then add to it what they learn about who lives at the park. Students decide what role they wish to play in preserving the aspects of the park that are significant to their lives. They may: write a letter requesting funding for clean-up; organize a community event; host a family picnic; research and work to conserve endangered species or habitats.	Art: sketch a particular place or tree; create a collage of images or photographs of the park Physical Education: engage in an activity that explores movements of various animals that live in the park; create an event for the class and the community

Notes:

Materials:

Time and Space:

CLASSROOM INTERACTIONS AND ROLES

The ecological approach puts exploration and experience at the heart of learning. The primary aim of the lesson is to explore and connect with local places and communities. As Demarest (2015) suggests, the curriculum should be responsive to local contexts, as well as connected to larger understandings of care and interconnectedness toward the aim of acting on one's beliefs. The objectives are often negotiated and collaborated upon by the teacher and students and are flexible to adapt to the evolving experience. The content is often inter- or multidisciplinary, but may not be, and includes identifiable knowledge and skills with associated meaning-making and action. Pedagogical approaches may take any form that is responsive to the needs of the investigation and to student learning. Students are actively involved in direct exploration of places while exploring ecomindedness through the content. Assessments are varied and may include pre-determined external tests, but more appropriately would include student self-evaluation of learning goals alongside the teacher's evaluation.

LESSON PLAN COMPARISON: THE ECOLOGICAL APPROACH TO TEACHING METAPHOR

While the single topic of metaphor might seem too narrow for an entire ecological lesson, this example shows that an ecominded experiential approach can work for even a limited topic or within a short timeframe. As we

Figure 6.5. Lesson Plan Comparison: Teaching Metaphor Through the Ecological Approach (Ecomindedness Integrated into Place-Based Design)

Teacher Thinking . . .	Students and Teacher Doing . . .
Lesson Plan Element: Investigative Questions	
How might I design experiences collaboratively with students that honor their past and present experiences? Some examples: Where are we? Who lives here? How did our community form? Where does our food come from? Where do we get our drinking water? What migration patterns exist in our communities?	Where do we find metaphors in literature and why? What metaphors are evident in the local schoolyard?
Experience-Based Objective	
What is the who, what, when, where, how, and why of the experience? Focus on the experience rather than the outcome. *What* concepts and skills will be explored? *How* will we design the experience to explore them? Involve students in creating the objective and attend to the personal, cultural, and social contexts of the lesson. *Who* will support students in their learning? *Where* and *when* will students engage with the content? Incorporate adaptable activities to support student interests. Describe and elicit from students the reasons for studying the concept. *Why* is this important? *How* does it connect to students' lives and promote future learning? What other content areas, learning experiences, and skill sets will emerge as significant after this lesson? How will students demonstrate their understandings and developing beliefs through a multiplicity of outcomes?	Students select books from home and from the library to find examples of metaphor. They search for physical metaphors in the schoolyard and create a list or narrative of their own. As the lesson progresses, students form organic groups to discuss how using metaphors about the schoolyard helps them think about caring for this place and how human interactions with objects lead to a deeper understanding of the collective meaning of this place.
Direct Exploration of Places and Development of a Sense of Place	
What opportunities exist for students to explore?	Using their own books and those selected from the library, students find several examples of metaphor. They discuss why authors use metaphor and what it adds to the literature.

Teacher Thinking . . .	Students and Teacher Doing . . .
	Students then explore the schoolyard for physical metaphors and create a list of their own. "The sidewalks are a web of journeys;" "The grass is a pillow for my dreams."
Multiple Pathways to Experience and Explore Ecomindedness, Including Caring, Interconnectedness, and Integrity	
What are the pathways to experience and explore caring, interconnectedness, and integrity?	*Care*: Students make small field journals from folded paper. Students talk with each other about how seeing the world in metaphors helps them think about its elements in a different way. *Interconnectedness*: After recording metaphors in their journals, students compare metaphors to see how they relate to enhance the way they see the schoolyard. *Integrity*: Given how our views of the schoolyard have been expanded, what might we do to take care of it?
Positive Action	
How can the students act to improve the situation being explored?	Discuss: Given how our views of the schoolyard have been expanded, what might we do to take care of it? The goal is that with an exploration of a literary concept in their local schoolyard, they will come to care in different ways for it, through both a greater understanding and appreciation, as well as for physical and practical care (throwing away trash, exploring new areas). They may choose from among the following or suggest something else: 1. Write a poem that uses an extended metaphor to explain the schoolyard's significance to them. 2. Write a letter to the school board requesting funds for a schoolyard improvement. Part of the letter could use metaphor or describe how this activity expanded their view of the schoolyard.

(continued)

Figure 6.5. Lesson Plan Comparison: Teaching Metaphor Through the Ecological Approach (Ecomindedness Integrated into Place-Based Design) ***(continued)***

Teacher Thinking . . .	Students and Teacher Doing . . .
Positive Action (continued)	
	3. Form a new club dedicated to schoolyard care. In the club's mission statement, use metaphor to communicate the significance of the schoolyard.
Inter- or Multidisciplinary Explorations	
How might I bring in interdisciplinary learning?	While this lesson is focused on English/ Language Arts, it could also be expanded to a study of communities and the schoolyard ecology if desired.

Materials: Books from home and the classroom, paper and staplers for making journals; materials available for projects as needed

Time and Space: Classroom, home, schoolyard; one class period plus time for projects

have said throughout the text, we encourage teachers to use these theories and ideas to unleash their own creativity. The lesson in Figure 6.5 is geared toward middle school but could be adapted to elementary or high school students.

CRITIQUES AND CONSIDERATIONS

The ecological approach to lesson planning is meant to break down many barriers—those between school and life, between nature and humans, and between the indoors and the out-of-doors. Further, the ecological approach is meant to help teachers who want to address environmental ideas but don't think they can take students outside or don't have the environmental literacy to design a lesson. Sometimes teachers simply think they don't have permission to teach environmental ideas. But the ecological approach can be local and place-based, or it can locate the content and identify where it lives—either of these approaches help students see relevance to their lives.

Critics of an ecological approach might argue that more emphasis is placed upon "non-tested" subjects and ideas, which is in fact a fair critique. However, we have seen through our work that when students find relevance, they are more motivated to extend and elaborate upon their learning, and the core concepts can still be at the heart of the experience.

Ecological Approach at a Glance

Rationale	Real-World Relevance and Connections
Theoretical Background	School should connect content and life so students can explore their local and global contexts toward the aim of ecological health and through the qualities of care, interconnectedness, and integrity
Practical Applications	Place-based curriculum design and ecomindedness; locate it, learn it, live it
Learning Aims	Experience-based objectives: who, what, when, where, why, and how will the students engage with the content?
Assessment and Evaluation	Core content within developing values and actions
Classroom Interactions	Exploration and experience with the opportunity to practice and perform care, interconnectedness, and integrity
Critiques and Considerations	Perceived challenges with going outside or on field trips or lack of teacher's knowledge of environmental concepts

Discussion Questions

1. What are the benefits and drawbacks of the ecological approaches to lesson planning and teaching?
2. What kinds of skills and knowledge in your content area are best suited to ecological lessons?
3. What kinds of skills and knowledge and understandings would be challenging to use in an ecological lesson?
4. What kinds of ecological lessons have you experienced? What do you like about them?
5. What are some educational experiences that ecological lessons cannot adequately address?

CHAPTER 7

The Integrated Social-Emotional Learning Approach to Lesson Planning

Relationship Building and Holistic Development

Social–emotional learning (SEL) has become increasingly important in light of the mental health pandemic facing children in the United States. According to the Centers for Disease Control (2019), childhood anxiety, depression, and suicide rates are at their highest in American history. One in five students (15 million) in the United States, aged 3–17, is suffering from some form of mental illness. Nearly half of all children in the United States, accounting for 34 million kids, suffer from trauma as a result of adverse childhood experiences (ACEs) such as abuse, poverty, substance abuse by a parent, and bullying (CAHMI, 2017; Jennings, 2018). Trauma adversely impacts brain development while also having tremendous psychological, physiological, and cognitive effects, making it difficult for students to adjust to the demands of school (Craig, 2008; Jennings, 2018). This current reality has led countless schools to turn their attention to integrating social–emotional learning into their curricula. Presently, every state has preschool social and emotional development standards, and 14 states have adopted K–12 social–emotional learning standards, with more expected to add them (Weissberg, Durlak, Domitrovich, & Gullotta, 2015).

The increased attention to social–emotional learning means that schools and teachers need to become more versed in incorporating SEL ideas in their curriculum. By incorporating perceptive teaching practices such as fostering safe, caring classrooms, providing choice through personalizing the educational experience, and helping students develop autonomy and feelings of success, teachers can create environments conducive to helping students suffering from trauma and mental health challenges to be more successful (National Child Traumatic Stress Network, 2008; We Are Teachers, 2020). We believe that the challenges our students face require multiple levels of support and intervention, within the school and outside of it. This chapter provides a lesson plan format that complements those efforts.

According to the Collaborative for Academic, Social, and Emotional Learning (CASEL), there are four primary ways that schools can implement social–emotional learning: (1) free-standing lessons; (2) general teaching practices; (3) integration; and (4) school-wide initiatives (Dusenbury, Calin, Domitrovich, & Weissberg, 2015). *Free-standing lessons* are characterized focused solely on social–emotional learning. *General teaching practices* refers to pedagogical approaches conducive to SEL (e.g., morning check-ins, advisory periods, cooperative group learning) though they may or may not specifically teach SEL concepts in their lessons. *Integration,* in the context of academic learning, means that the teacher will teach SEL skills alongside subject matter content within a lesson. *School-wide initiatives* occur when an entire school structures itself—from organizational, operational, curricular, and pedagogical standpoints—to focus on social–emotional learning goals.

While social–emotional learning can be implemented as a stand-alone lesson on a topic such as empathy, through general teaching practices, or as schoolwide undertakings, in this chapter we focus on social–emotional learning as an integration of SEL concepts in the academic curriculum. We can incorporate practicing empathy in any lesson. Later, we use the term Integrated Social Emotional Lesson planning (ISEL) in a nod to CASEL's integration approach, but we specify and clarify a particular lesson planning approach not previously articulated. That is, ISEL is our creation.

An integrated social–emotional approach to learning teaches both academic and social–emotional skills within a single lesson plan. The subject matter is often mediated by the SEL skill being taught, thereby enhancing the academic understanding and meaning (Durlak, Weissberg, Dymnicki, Taylor, & Schellinger, 2011). Subject matter content as well as social–emotional content is explicitly introduced, taught, and then reflected upon in a lesson. The overall structure of such a lesson includes a brief inclusion activity introducing both academic and social–emotional content to be covered in the lesson, a body of the lesson focused on engaging practices, and a space at the end of the lesson intentionally concentrated on reflection.

Learning objectives for integrated social–emotional lesson plans are written to include both an academic and a social component. Students also can write their own social–emotional learning objective for the lesson, week, or month; this provides them with choice and voice. Also unique to this approach is the intentional space created for reflection at the end of the lesson. In this space, referred to as an optimistic closure, teachers intentionally create opportunities for students to discuss what they have learned, to understand their thinking, to make meaningful connections to their lives, and to look ahead to where they will go.

RATIONALE

In addition to addressing mental and emotional health crises, integrated SEL curriculum can help students maximize their academic potential by ensuring they are fully engaged in learning: cognitively, emotionally, and socially. SEL has also been shown to lead to students feeling happier and more fulfilled in the school environment (Durlak et al., 2011). Teachers can rethink classroom management, pedagogy, and curriculum through the lens of teaching the whole child. Further, SEL helps students develop a growth mindset, helping them stay motivated, set goals, and develop autonomy. The integrated approach, which we discuss in this chapter, is not an add-on that will simply take more time. Rather, it is an invitation to consider curriculum planning through and with social–emotional awareness embedded in content.

THEORETICAL BACKGROUND

While the term *social–emotional learning* may be relatively new, the concept has deep roots in the field of holistic education. Three seminal mid-19th century educators (John Dewey, Maria Montessori, and Rudolf Steiner) each drew attention to holistic education through their extensive writings and the schools that they founded (the Chicago Lab School, Montessori schools, and Waldorf schools, respectively). In the 1960s and 1970s a number of alternative schools utilized holistic styles of education (see Gross & Gross, 1969). More recently, James Comer (1980) examined how students' home and school lives affect their academic lives. In this work, he created and implemented the Comer Process in two schools, illustrating that attending to the social and emotional elements of a student's life can lead to much improved academic success. Later in 1997, CASEL partnered with the Association for Supervision and Curriculum Development (ASCD) to create *Promoting Social and Emotional Learning: Guidelines for Educators*. This book, describing ways in which schools and teachers could implement an SEL program, led to a growing desire for schools to incorporate social–emotional learning into their curricula.

Social–emotional learning is rooted in the notion that intelligence is not solely linked to the cognitive domain, which is the domain upon which standards, school curricula, and most student outcomes are based. Much in line with Howard Gardner's (1983) theory of multiple intelligences, those who advocate for SEL argue that there is more than one kind of intelligence, and that along with the cognitive, we must also attend to social and emotional intelligences. The belief that there are multiple types of intelligence has a longstanding history in the field, dating as far back as its inception (Salovey & Mayer, 1990). E. L. Thorndike (1920) is credited with first introducing the notion of social intelligence, which diverged from cognitive intelligence in that it was focused on one's ability to understand and manage people and to "act wisely in human relations" (p. 228). While the definition of social intelligence has certainly evolved over time, the basic notion, referring to one's ability to understand and effectively navigate diverse human situations, remains.

Emotional intelligence is a subset of social intelligence (Salovey & Mayer, 1990). Salovey and Mayer argued that emotional intelligence is on par with cognitive intelligence. They write: "Emotional intelligence involves the ability to monitor one's own and others' feelings and emotions, to discriminate among them and to use this information to guide one's thinking and actions" (p. 189). Soon after, Daniel Goleman's book *Emotional Intelligence: Why It Can Matter More than IQ* (1995) was published for a general audience. It became a bestseller and led to vigorous academic work in this area (Mayer, Salovey, Caruso, & Cherkasskiy, 2011). While working on his best-selling book, Goleman joined a small group of educators and researchers to found The Collaborative for Academic, Social, and Emotional Learning (CASEL), which currently stands as the foremost authority in social–emotional learning, a term that first emerged during the organization's founding in 1994 (CASEL, "History," n.d.).

CASEL now defines SEL as "the process through which children and adults understand and manage emotions, set and achieve positive goals, feel and show empathy for others, establish and maintain positive relationships, and make responsible decisions" (CASEL, 2019). Elias and his colleagues add that SEL includes active learning, transferrable skills, and the development of one's ability to apply social decisionmaking and problem-solving skills in a multitude of situations. Further, SEL aims to "help students develop the attitudes, behaviors, and cognitions to become 'healthy and competent' overall—socially, emotionally, academically, and physically—because of the close relationship among these domains" (Elias, Zins, & Weissberg, 1997, p. 2).

Only recently has the impact of social–emotional learning been examined. In a monumental study, Durlak and his colleagues did a meta-analysis of 213 social–emotional programs involving over 270,000 K–12 students and found that these students showed significant improvement in their social and emotional skills, behaviors, attitudes, and even academic performance. Further, the study found that those students had fewer behavioral conduct problems while the schools in which the programs were implemented reported less acts of aggression or acts that resulted in school punishment (Durlak et al., 2011). In a follow-up study examining longitudinal research of over 97,000 K–12 students, Taylor and his colleagues found that the students showed significant improvement in social and emotional skills, academic achievement, and higher graduation rates (Taylor, Oberle, Durlak, & Weissberg, 2017). Two other studies yielded similar findings, illustrating that students who engage in SEL curricula showed increased gains in social–emotional skills and academic achievement compared to similar students who did not (Sklad, Diekstra, De Ritter, Ben, & Gravesteijn, 2012; Wiglesworth et al., 2016).

Research has further indicated that children with poor social–emotional skills tend to struggle academically, have a greater distaste for school, and are more likely to be retained or drop out completely (Raver & Knitzer, 2002). One study found that SEL led to decreased bullying and victimization (Nickerson, 2018; Nickerson, Fredrick, Allen, & Jenkins, 2019) while still another found it led to decreased incidents of aggressive and violent behavior (Ttofi, Bowes, Farrington, & Lösel, 2014). Research also has indicated that SEL has a positive effect on students suffering from the effects of trauma (Darling-Hammond & Cook-Harvey, 2018; Ward-Roncalli, 2018). The growing body of research supporting increased social–emotional learning in schools have led experts such as Linda Darling-Hammond (2015) to proclaim, "The survival of the human race depends at least as much on the cultivation of social and emotional intelligence as it does on the development of technical knowledge and skills" (p. xi).

Though the early research indicates that social–emotional learning produces many positive results, much more work remains in developing this approach. In particular, much needs to be done to provide teachers the tools to write, implement, and evaluate integrated SEL lesson plans. Unlike the other approaches, integrated social–emotional learning intentionally aims to attend to both the cognitive and the affective domains of learning. The goal of integrated SEL is to teach the whole child, with a view that a socially and emotionally well-adjusted child is better prepared to thrive academically, much as Comer's work indicated. This approach increases the likelihood for student buy-in, engagement, and holistic growth.

PRACTICAL APPLICATION: LESSON PLAN FORMATS

Only a few models exist for the Integrated Social Emotional lesson plan approach. More common are prewritten curricula that can be implemented across the school and in the classroom. Examples of these include *Connect Learning*, *Second Step*, *Roots of Empathy*, and *Character Strong*. Of the models in which teachers can write their own curriculum, CASEL offers a number of sample lessons and a myriad of resources. A model curriculum offered by Meena Srinivasan (2018) is called *SEL Everyday*. This text offers teachers a detailed, four-part, 8-page model that includes identifying desired results, gathering evidence of those results, a multipart lesson plan body, and a space for teacher reflection and student feedback. *SEL Everyday* is special in that it offers teachers a framework in which to plan, though admittedly it is quite long and may be time-consuming to complete. Each of these curricula include social and emotional as well as academic learning objectives/foci, and each incorporates CASEL's three signature practices for

SEL: an inclusion activity, engaging practices, and optimistic closure (described in more detail later) (CASEL, 2019).

LEARNING AIMS: INTEGRATED SOCIAL-EMOTIONAL AND INDIVIDUAL SEL OBJECTIVES

Similarly, the Integrated Social–Emotional lesson plan approach offered here explicitly incorporates social–emotional learning into each daily lesson plan while remaining focused on academic learning. ISEL lesson plans contain objectives with both an academic and a social–emotional component, written in ABC format and in student-friendly language. Along with the integrated social–emotional objective, students create a social–emotional objective for themselves for the lesson, week, or month on which they can track their progress. In this approach, academic content is mediated through social–emotional experiences. Such experiences are shared with classmates, which leads to co-construction of meaning. Students draw upon their own experiences as well as the experiences of others to make meaning of content while developing their own social–emotional skills.

The Integrated Social–Emotional Lesson plan approach offers a template that employs the CASEL's three signature practices of SEL learning as a backdrop: inclusion activity, engaging practices, and optimistic closure. An *inclusion activity* is an opening activity, ritual, or routine that aims to build community while connecting to the content that will be covered. Examples include morning circles, community meanings, or paired discussions.

Engaging practices are pedagogical approaches where teachers create spaces for learning, discussion, and engagement with the content. These spaces support both group and individual learning, balancing reflective and interactive experiences for students, thus attending to inter- and intrapersonal intelligences. Examples include pair-shares, jigsaw activities, and mindful minute brain breaks.

Finally, optimistic closures are spaces reserved for the end of the lessons to give students time to reflect, make connections, and think about next steps in their academic and social–emotional learning. Examples of optimistic closures include writing exit tickets about three things they learned; a turn and talk about something they learned and a connection they made; and a think–write–pair-share responding to a prompt about how the social–emotional skill helped them in the process of learning the content.

As a whole, the ISEL model is comprised of four primary elements:

1. Integrated social–emotional objectives & student SEL objective
2. Inclusion activity
3. Body with engaging practices
4. Optimistic closure

To begin writing an ISEL lesson, teachers identify the academic content they will teach in a lesson and then pinpoint at least one social–emotional skill they will focus on for the lesson, week, or even month, with the latter ideally developed in tandem with the students (Srinivasan, 2018). The skills are written in an integrated fashion with both academic and SEL objectives incorporated into a single objective. An example of an integrated objective might be something like, "We can collaborate with a small group to analyze one cause of the Civil War by creating a cause and effect chart on a poster." Here the teacher is focusing on the SEL skill of working collaboratively and the academic objective of analyzing one cause of the Civil War. Some teachers might find it easier to first write their academic objective(s), then write their SEL objective(s), before combining them into an integrated SEL objective. Regardless of the creation method, teachers should be explicit in sharing the objectives with students both verbally and in writing (e.g., displayed on a whiteboard). The teacher should explicitly share the SEL skill to be developed with students.

It is important for teachers to develop SEL objectives with an equity lens so as not to inadvertently reinforce implicit power and privilege inequities. Teachers can also invite students to write a social–emotional learning objective for themselves that might cover a single lesson or a longer period such as a week, month, or year.

Teachers generally have access to the academic curriculum in the form of district, building, or school-level curricula (e.g., scope and sequence guides), but if their state or school has not yet adopted SEL standards, they can draw on CASEL's Five Core Social Emotional Competencies (CASEL, n.d.) (see Figure 7.1). These competencies include self-awareness, self-management, social awareness, relationship skills, and responsible decisionmaking.

Self-awareness refers to one's ability to identify, and reflect on their thoughts, abilities, emotions, values, and behaviors. Examples of self-awareness include identifying emotions, accurate self-perception, recognizing strengths, and self-efficacy.

Self-management refers to one's ability to regulate emotions, thoughts and behaviors, to manage stress, to motivate oneself, and to manage impulsivity. Examples of self-management include impulse control, stress management, self-discipline, self-motivation, goal-setting, and organizational skills.

Social awareness refers to the ability to see through various perspectives and to value diverse cultures. Examples of social awareness include perspective-taking, empathy, appreciating diversity, and respect for others.

Relationship skills refer to one's ability to establish and maintain positive relationships with diverse people and groups, to communicate, cooperate, and listen to others, and to resist negative social pressures. Examples of relationships skills include communication, social engagement, sharing thoughts and feelings appropriately, relationship building, and teamwork.

Finally, ***responsible decisionmaking*** refers to one's ability to make choices that take into consideration one's own as well as others' well-being. Examples of responsible decisionmaking include identifying problems, analyzing situations, solving problems, evaluating, reflecting, and ethical responsibility.

These five elements can comprise the SEL portion of the objective. Teachers can collaboratively select social–emotional goals with the students to integrate the social–emotional focus with the academic objectives within the lesson before designing learning experiences. For example, if the teacher and students decide to focus on goal-setting for the week while studying ratios in math class, the teacher might write an objective such as "We will be able to calculate the ratio of various objects in 10 different word problems by solving them with my group and completing all 10 accurately by tomorrow's deadline." In this example, the academic element of the objective is the calculating of ratios in 10 different word problems, and the SEL component include goals of getting them accurate and getting the work turned in on time.

Teachers might also at this point invite students to create their own social–emotional objective, deciding ahead of time how long students will be focusing on their individual SEL objectives (a day, week, month, etc.). It would be wise for teachers to determine how they are going to have their students track their progress on the objectives—for example, having students log their work on a chart or in a journal.

Teachers do not have to be social–emotional experts to explicitly integrate SEL into their lesson plans; they may simply use the above five elements. The Integrated Social Emotional Lesson Plan model is designed to help teachers more intentionally build social–emotional concepts into lessons alongside subject matter content. It is important to note that all learning is inherently social and emotional, whether we attend to those qualities of the learning experience or not. The Integrated Social Emotional Lesson Plan model helps teachers be more explicit in their teaching of social–emotional skills.

Once the objectives are in place, the teacher can turn to the inclusion activity. Much like the anticipatory set in the Hunter model or the enroll in the EEL DR C model, the inclusion activity is designed to hook students, but it further invites students' voices into the room, developing their interpersonal skills, and connects to the content that will be covered that day. The opening activity should include sharing with students the objective(s) for the day, and at times can be a place for students to offer input on the SEL component of the objectives or to develop their own objectives. Moreover, the engagement activity serves as a place where teachers can establish, nurture, and grow their classroom environment as inclusive, safe, valuing of diversity, and anchored on academic as well as social–emotional learning. Inclusion activities can be shortened at times to include more traditional pedagogical approaches that incorporate SEL, such as a four-corner activity that attends to content while focusing on situation analysis, evaluating, perspective-taking, and empathy. In such an activity, students go to one of four corners in the room based on their opinion of a certain statement (strongly agree, agree, disagree, strongly disagree) and articulate with other students why they hold that position. Other times, inclusion activities might attend more specifically to social–emotional learning, such as an activity where students walk around the room for 3–5 minutes to make a connection with as many people as they can, thus focusing on the skill of social engagement and relationship building.

The body of the ISEL lesson includes at least one engaging practice that promotes SEL (e.g., pair-share, jigsaw, Socratic Seminar, etc.). Engaging practices are designed to support both individual and collaborative learning and include processing/reflection time as well as highly engaging pedagogical methods. There are myriad pedagogical practices prescribed to foster social–emotional learning within the classroom. While the list is too exhaustive to include here, choose strategies that have the following criteria:

1. The activity promotes high engagement, meaning students are present and participating.
2. The activity promotes inclusivity and equity.
3. Students collaborate with others for at least part of the time.
4. There are moments for creating, evaluating, reflecting, and sharing.
5. Students are moving about for all or part of the activity rather than being sequestered in desks.
6. There are brain breaks to process information, make connections, and increase transfer.

Some popular examples of the above include cooperative learning, which encourages key SEL skills such as listening, teamwork, and relationship building (VanAusdal, 2019). Other strategies include discussion, drawing, writing, implementing SEL handouts, role-play, and skill practice activities (CASEL, 2017), which were found to intentionally develop SEL skills.

The final stage of the ISEL lesson plan is optimistic closure, which is similar to the Hunter evaluation and closure and the EEL DR C celebrate. The optimistic closure is a time for students to reflect on the work done in class that day, to look ahead, possibly to summarize their thinking (e.g., via exit ticket), and/or to make connections to their lives and/or other school work. Optimistic closures are a space for bringing forth the individual as well as the shared understanding of the importance of what was learned in class, academic and social–emotional (CASEL, 2019). Optimistic closures provide students opportunity to make meaning, connect learning to their own lives, and to build anticipation for what will come next.

Further, the closures let teachers help students build their metacognition skills by providing a space for them to think about the academic content and the social–emotional skills being learned. The three stages described above—selecting whole-class and individual objectives, participating in engaging activities, and ending with optimistic closure—support an appreciation for academic and social–emotional learning as valuable to success and happiness in school and in life.

Included in Figure 7.1 are the five social–emotional competencies with several examples of elements that comprise those competencies. Within the parenthesis are sample activities teachers might employ to help develop those social–emotional skills.

ASSESSMENT AND EVALUATION

Because academic and SEL learning are integrated, the assessments may take many forms. A lesson on ratios could simply include a demonstration of learning the academic content: Do students understand how to calculate ratios? In a cooperative learning situation, students may need to demonstrate they not only understand ratios, but that they can work collaboratively on related problems. SEL evaluation is highly personalized, and teachers and students may collaborate to discuss ways they want to demonstrate competencies and growth, including peer interviews, journaling, parent conferences, and social–emotional tracking activities. Again, by creating individualized social–emotional objectives, students themselves can track their growth on the skills on which they are focusing, which is a form of developing autonomy (see the perceptive teaching framework).

Teachers who are interested in a more formalized evaluation of SEL may access specific assessments from the CASEL SEL Assessment guide (available online at measuringsel.casel.org/assessment-guide/) and the RAND Assessment Finder (www.rand.org/education-and-labor/projects/assessments.html). These assessments can be used diagnostically, formatively, or summatively to monitor student progress on SEL goals or competencies (Taylor et al., 2018). There are various types of SEL assessments teachers can utilize, each of which has its advantages and disadvantages. Many of these tools are qualitative and include assessments such as surveys or questionnaires, interviews, or observations. Teachers can also employ performance-based assessments designed to create authentic situations where students are asked to apply social–emotional skills. Other assessments such as the Devereux Student Strengths Assessment (DESSA)

Figure 7.1. Five Social-Emotional Competencies

are more qualitative, serving as a standardized, norm-referenced behavior rating scale designed to assess social and emotional competencies. The assessment of so-called soft skills has proven challenging, but a great deal of work is being undertaken in this area to provide more data. Some schools have created their own SEL assessments, such as the Nueva School in California, which uses "habits of learning" rubrics to assess students' SEL competencies (Curtis, 2017).

Given the link researchers have identified between SEL competencies and student achievement, teachers can also use outcome measures (e.g., academic measures) to assess growth and effectiveness of SEL content. Teachers can employ an integrative assessment approach by adding social–emotional questions or prompts to academic assessments to diagnostically, formatively, or summatively assess student growth and learning of the SEL skills covered in class. In school- or district-wide SEL program implementations, teachers can link classroom SEL content with school or district content to reinforce the learning. Teachers must again think about SEL assessment through an equity lens and remember that if they assess items or tasks that are "heavily influenced by values of a dominant culture, but may not be shared by other cultures, the results of the assessment may fail to capture strengths and perspectives of students from all cultures" (Taylor et al., 2018, p. 7).

At the school or district level, educators and researchers can employ either outcomes assessments or process assessments (Minnesota Dept. of Education, 2018). Outcomes assessments are designed to assess the "competencies, attitudes and perceptions that you hope to improve as a result of SEL-related efforts" and can be drawn from existing data such as student GPA, attendance, graduation rates, and behavioral incidences (Minnesota Dept. of Education, 2018, p. 5). Process measures are employed to check the effectiveness of practices, programs, and interventions at the school or district level and include data from items such as surveys or observations (Minnesota Dept. of Education, 2018).

CLASSROOM INTERACTIONS AND ROLES

In taking a more holistic view of educating students, the integrated social–emotional approach attends to the cognitive as well as the affective domains of learning. In doing so, teachers are intentional about getting to know their students as people as well as pupils. Teachers employ a pedagogical approach that is more student centered, interactive, and engaging while ensuring intermittent brain breaks for processing of academic and/or social–emotional content. Students are empowered to have input on integrated social–emotional objectives as well as individual social–emotional objectives at appropriate times. Students who are successful in classrooms utilizing an integrated social–emotional approach are self-reflective, collaborative, and active in the learning process.

LESSON PLAN COMPARISON: THE INTEGRATED SOCIAL-EMOTIONAL LEARNING APPROACH TO TEACHING METAPHOR

In our final example of teaching metaphor using our models (Figure 7.2), we focus on two academic and two social–emotional elements. Much as we did in the constructivist lesson plan example of teaching metaphor in a high school, the academic component of the objectives in the ISEL example is identifying and analyzing metaphor. Unlike the constructivist example, we are also going to focus on the social–emotional skills of sharing one's thoughts and feelings as well as contributing to the achievement of a group. Juxtaposing the ISEL and constructivist models could be instructive in helping you see similarities and differences in these two models.

Figure 7.2. Integrated Social-Emotional Lesson Plan: Teaching Metaphor

Teacher Thinking . . .	Students and Teacher Doing . . .
	Lesson Plan Element: Integrated Social–Emotional Objective & Student SEL Objective
What academic content am I going to cover? What SEL skill(s) will I focus on? How can I create social–emotional experiences to help students mediate the content? What kinds of personalized objectives am I hoping students will create?	Students are going to be able to identify and analyze metaphors in prose, to identify *imagery*, and by sharing their thoughts and feelings appropriately and working in a group, to achieve the goal of evaluating at least 3-5 metaphors in Ralph Ellison's *Invisible Man*. *Academic Content:* Students will identify and analyze metaphor *SEL Skill:* Share ones' thoughts and feelings appropriately and contribute to the achievement of group goals (effective collaboration) Have students record their own personalized SEL objective and share with the teacher.
	Inclusion Activity
How can I engage the students and invite their voices into the room? What interpersonal skill can we incorporate and how might I connect that to the academic content we will cover today?	Share with the students that today they are going to learn to identify and analyze the imagery in poetry. To do this they are going to focus on the skills of sharing their thoughts and feelings appropriately and contributing to the achievement of group goals. Play the video animation of Paul Laurence Dunbar's reading of his poem "Sympathy." Ask the students to listen. Then give them a handout of the poem's text. Replay the audio and ask the students to follow along and identify any images created. Ask students to share what they found with a partner. Then invite them to share with the whole class.
	Body of Lesson with Engaging Practices
How am I promoting SEL? Where can we draw upon each other's experiences to make meaning? Does my lesson meet the following criteria: The activity promotes high engagement, meaning students are present and participating. Students collaborate with others for at least part of the time. There are moments for creating, evaluating, reflecting, and sharing.	Provide a brief minilesson on imagery and metaphor and what they reveal about a speaker. Explain the definition and purpose of each and share that metaphors not only compare unlike things without using like or as, they create images. Also explain that the references to metaphors reveal things about the speaker. Ask the students, in groups of three, to circle metaphors they see in "Sympathy." Ask students to describe the images created by the metaphors and what they reveal about the speaker on a three-column chart. Confer with students, formatively assess, and ensure they are working as a team to complete the three-column chart while appropriately sharing their thoughts and feelings.

Teacher Thinking . . .	Students and Teacher Doing . . .
There are moments for creating, evaluating, reflecting, and sharing. Students are moving about for all or part of the activity rather than being sequestered in desks. Brain breaks are provided to process information, make connections, and increase transfer.	Give the students a longer excerpt of Ralph Ellison's *Invisible Man*. Invite the students to collaborate as a team of three to fill out the three-column chart for the text, where they identify 3–5 metaphors. For at least one of the metaphors/images they select, ask the students to each write a 2–5 sentence response to the following prompt: Select a metaphor that you connected with and describe how you felt, as the narrator in the story did. What image came to mind for you when you felt that way? Share that their goal is to collaboratively fill out the three-column chart and to write a response to the prompt to be turned in at the end of the class period. Briefly discuss as a whole group what good collaboration looks like. Record answers on the board. Be sure to elicit from them that good collaboration includes sharing, clear communication, good listening, problem solving, support, and embracing diverse perspectives. After individually checking in with students, invite them to share their response to the prompt with each other.
	Optimistic Closure
How will I have students reflect on their learning in an engaging way? How will they capture their thinking and allow me to formatively assess their learning? Where can they make connections between the academic/SEL content and their lives? How will we look ahead to what's to come?	Ask the students to pair-share how they have made sense of struggle and inequality in their own lives. End with a high five or handshake. On an exit ticket, ask the students to respond to the following: 1. What is imagery? 2. What can metaphor reveal about a speaker? 3. How did you effectively express your feelings and thoughts today? What was challenging? 4. What elements of good collaboration did your group exhibit today? How might your group improve? 5. Describe your progress on meeting your personal SEL objective. Share with the students what they will be doing next period and reiterate that what they are learning in this unit is helping them on their way to writing literary analysis essays.

Materials: Dunbar video (www.youtube.com/watch?v=5eDpNcJ0-qo), "Sympathy" poem lyrics, *Invisible Man* excerpt, three-column charts

Time and Space: One class period, classroom space with positive messaging on walls

CRITIQUES AND CONSIDERATIONS

In our work with educators across the country, we frequently hear the following:

- SEL curricula feel irrelevant because they don't reflect students' experiences, and may oversimplify or ignore the real challenges students face in their everyday lives.
- There is not enough time for SEL because of competing academic priorities.
- Teachers and staff do not receive enough professional development and support to implement SEL programs successfully or to engage in their own authentic social–emotional growth.
- Rigid lesson plans don't allow teachers to respond to students' evolving needs.

Some have criticized SEL for enforcing White, normative behavior, though organizations such as CASEL are explicit in urging teachers to be conscious of this possibility and guard against it. We believe that teachers who study and practice culturally responsive teaching and the qualities of perceptive teaching as explored in Chapter 2 can avoid these pitfalls.

Many traditional SEL programs consist of scripted and sequenced curricula that are designed to be used in a weekly 30-minute block, often led by a school counselor or designated SEL facilitator. They tend to be expensive, require significant training and ongoing support, and limit individual autonomy or choice, as adaptations or deviations from the script are seen as threats to program fidelity. While these programs are an important option, schools may have difficulty implementing them as intended, integrating them throughout the day and across multiple settings, and sustaining them over time. Such prescriptive approaches also fail to leverage the expertise of teachers who ultimately know their classroom best, and whose relationships, observations, and decisions are critical to providing effective and timely social–emotional support for students. There is a pressing need for an approach to SEL that is more flexible and feasible to implement, and adaptable to individual and place-based needs, while still achieving meaningful outcomes for children (Jones et al., 2017).

As with other approaches, there are many considerations about when and how to design curriculum with an integrated SEL lens. Some teachers may feel ill equipped to handle the social–emotional needs of students; they are typically not licensed counselors. Teachers may also not yet be convinced that social–emotional learning can enhance academic learning. We invite teachers to try this and the other models to see what the results are in their own classrooms—what happens to classroom management? How are the relationships with students developing? How are students interacting with each other? What is the climate in the classroom? Trying out various ISEL lessons will provide an interesting perspective on teaching and learning.

The Integrated Social-Emotional Approach at a Glance

Rationale	Relationship Building and Holistic Development
Theoretical Background	Teachers teach the whole child, helping students grow intellectually, socially, and emotionally.
Practical Applications	Integrated Social–Emotional model
Learning Aims	Integrated Social–Emotional Objectives: One academic skill and one social–emotional skill Individualized Social–Emotional Objective: One SEL skill created by students
Assessment and Evaluation	Qualitative assessments, performance assessments, demonstration of content understanding, personalized self-evaluation, student achievement measures
Classroom Interactions	Teachers get to know students as people and pupils, using engaging pedagogical practices with brain breaks. Students work collaboratively and individually, encouraged to be self-reflective.
Critiques and Considerations	May feel irrelevant; not enough time in the school day; lack of professional development; can encourage White, normative behavior; teachers may be ill-prepared to teach SEL.

Discussion Questions

1. Why does social-emotional learning matter?
2. How can you adapt your lesson plans to incorporate social-emotional learning?
3. What are the challenges to implementing social-emotional learning?
4. What professional development could help you in writing integrated social-emotional lesson plans?
5. How does drawing upon your own or others' experiences help you make meaning?
6. What are the benefits and shortcomings of writing integrated social-emotional objectives vs. academic ones and social-emotional ones?
7. In what other ways might we help our students in tracking progress on individual SEL objectives?

CHAPTER 8

Planning with Purpose Summary and Extensions

Welcome to the last chapter of the book. Some of you arrived here by skipping around from one chapter to another. Some of you read each chapter in order. And some of you have flipped to the back pages to see how it all wraps up before starting your journey through the book itself. Whatever the case, we offer a summary of some key points of the text and then extensions of the ideas discussed to help you think about how you might integrate ideas from multiple approaches into a single lesson or a single approach across an entire unit.

THE FIVE APPROACHES TO LESSON PLANNING

Teaching is a complex activity with many demands placed on it. While there are a variety of reasons why someone may end up in the teaching profession, we think that for most the desire to create meaningful educational experiences for students is primary. The question is how to do that when faced with so many challenges. Our goal has been to help you stay focused on what is paramount: student growth and learning. We offered five approaches to lesson planning: behaviorist, constructivist, aesthetic, ecological, and integrated social–emotional. Unlike numerous trends and pendulum swings in education that champion a one-best-method, we have argued that there are various approaches to lesson planning, and each of the five mentioned in this book has its own value in different times and places (see Figure 8.1). Teachers need to decide which method(s) fit their needs and interests in specific contexts throughout the year.

We believe that the ***behaviorist approach*** is fitting when teachers want to develop well-defined skills, perhaps two-digit addition or writing a thesis statement. A behaviorist lesson plan (the Hunter Model) is best employed when the teacher has a clear idea of exactly what they would like their students to produce. To achieve this aim, the teacher will model the behavior and outcome while closely guiding students through the activity before

Figure 8.1. Comparison of Lesson Plan Approaches

Behaviorist	Constructivist	Aesthetic	Ecological	Integrated Social–Emotional
Skill Development	Individualized Meaning-Making	Sensory-rich, memorable experiences	Real-world relevance and connections	Relationship building and holistic development

allowing them to work independently. We note that students who are considered to be "struggling" may benefit from this direct approach, but they should not be limited to it; all students deserve to experience a variety of methods so they can make meaning of their learning.

The ***constructivist approach*** is particularly useful when teachers want to assist students in making meaning out of the content, such as "What does freedom mean to you?" A constructivist lesson plan (EEL DR C) is useful when teachers want student-centered lessons geared toward higher-level thinking and individualized meaning-making. The practice of having students experience learning before naming it found in EEL DR C can be particularly helpful in keeping students from being overwhelmed or intimidated by complex, or at least complex-sounding, content. For instance, we have used this lesson plan model to teach rhetorical analysis. Rather than tell the students, "Today you are going to do rhetorical analysis by examining, analyzing, and writing three types of parallelism," we gave them an experience with it, showed them that it was something they could do, and then labeled what they did.

The ***aesthetic approach*** reminds teachers that students will remember and enjoy sensory-rich activities. We bet that many of you can remember K–12 experiences that were out of the ordinary and that were particularly engaging. For example, a lesson in which students use arithmetic in a class candy store—setting up the store initially, adding items, making change—makes the math fun and memorable. An aesthetic lesson plan (CRISPA) not only enhances the likelihood that students will be engaged, it can break the monotony for teachers of using recycled lessons that they have taught for years. For new teachers, using CRISPA from the start begins their practice with exciting and memorable ways to explore content that avoids skill-and-drill lessons that may bore their students.

The ***ecological approach*** focuses on place and real-world connections. Students could practice their two-digit addition outside the classroom, perhaps on the playground. Students could count flowers, fence links, or grass blades. Whatever the case, they can learn about their surroundings along with learning about addition. Such awareness can lead them to develop a sense of place and relationship with their schoolyard, which sets the stage for deeper care. An ecological lesson plan (place-based or ecominded) can be used in any content area and assists teachers in helping students find relevance in the content and see connections to their world.

Finally, the ***integrated social–emotional approach*** reminds educators to teach to the whole child and to pay attention to relationships. This approach may encourage a teacher to have students learn linear equations by calculating how states determine how much to charge for a speeding ticket. Teachers could ask students how they would regulate their emotions if they were put in a tense situation, such as being pulled over for speeding. An integrated social–emotional lesson plan (ISEL) can be used in any content area but calls for teachers to provide engaging experiences with both academic *and* social–emotional content.

Each of the five approaches encourages teachers to think in different ways. Each approach focuses on some items unique to that approach, and each approach leaves out some ideas and thinking that may be highlighted in other approaches. Hence all five are important if we want our students to have more meaningful experiences in schools and more diverse skills for life.

PAYING ATTENTION TO CONTEXT: PERCEPTIVE TEACHING

We have also noted that planning with purpose means that we must pay attention to context. In order to create rich learning spaces, we need to get to know individual students so that we can understand how to engage them in the lessons we teach. Understanding students' cultures is a good start, and we must also examine and understand our own culture. Culturally responsive pedagogy (CRP) aims to create equitable classrooms by empowering ethnically diverse students to learn through a rigorous curriculum that meets their interests and needs. CRP provides an asset model that focuses on students' cultural knowledge, talents, and experiences that should be included to create meaningful learning environments. As a complement to CRP, through a literature review and our own research, we described a number of qualities that we believe teachers should develop: open-mindedness, a heightened sense of awareness, caring, authenticity, personalizing the educational experience, teaching the whole person, teaching with intention, and developing autonomy. When these qualities are developed and actualized, teachers acknowledge, embrace, and help sustain students' complex identities. We call it *perceptive teaching,* the process through which teachers continually reflect upon, learn about, and adapt their teaching practices to meet the needs of their students as they engage in an exploration of rigorous and relevant content.

BLENDING APPROACHES

To this point we have treated each of the five lesson plans as a stand-alone model, providing a framework for you to create them with the assistance of prompts as you learn each approach. For example, you learned each step of an EEL DR C lesson and we encouraged you to include each element of that framework—enroll, experience, label, demonstrate, review, and celebrate. Our aim in examining each approach separately is to help you both understand the unique elements of each lesson plan approach and to assist you in developing habits of mind when lesson planning.

As you have explored each approach, you may have seen places where they could overlap or even complement one another. As you develop in your planning with these models, you can draw upon elements of each to blend them into a single lesson. In fact, we encourage you to blend the various approaches as you see fit. For example, we noted in the aesthetic approach that this method can be used as an overlay to any other approach. That is, CRISPA can be applied to all the other methods. As a quick example, you could think about providing sensory experiences or risk-taking in a constructivist, an ecological, or an integrated social–emotional lesson plan. And when doing so, you are providing opportunities for students to have aesthetic—wow—experiences. When writing an integrated social–emotional lesson, the "body with engaging practices" portion could be designed with any of the four lesson plan approaches. In fact, the ISEL lesson is left intentionally open for teacher creativity and responsiveness to student needs. For some, that metaphorical blank slate is a welcome gift. For others, it can be overwhelming and having the structure offered in, say, the Hunter model can be helpful.

Further, we can cherry-pick single elements from the various approaches in creating blended lesson plans. For example, we might write an ecological lesson plan where students explore some element of their immediate surroundings. In the lesson, we might allow time to create meaning through an experience (see EEL DR C), or we might provide them a model of something we want them to do along with practice time (see the Hunter model). First, students might learn a topic through meaning-making, but then some drill and practice might be a good idea—students could memorize 10 local wildflowers to enhance their knowledge of place. Likewise, the integrated social–emotional approach could be utilized with any other approach and it would remind educators to attend to, as the name implies, social and emotional growth and learning along with the cognitive.

Stated metaphorically, these lesson plan models may be thought of as five approaches to purposeful planning in your artist's palette. Colors are vibrant on their own, but they can become exciting and stimulating when blended. As you practice each form and design lessons for your students, you will begin to develop a unique teaching identity that includes powerful tools for engaged learning.

ANOTHER WORD ON LESSON PLANNING

Throughout this book we have described what goes into lesson plan design and thinking. We have spent less time, however, on explaining what an actual lesson plan looks like in all of its material glory. By this time, you have clearly figured out that a lesson plan could be expressed in chart form (as we have provided in each chapter); the templates are demonstrations of thinking and planning. Several of us use this method with preservice teachers. But a lesson plan could take other formats, including those prescribed by a school, district, or university. The five approaches are adaptable to a variety of required structures. For example, some schools may require that teachers list all of the standards addressed, and we have included in this book standards-referenced lessons while not explicitly providing a required space to note them. See Figure 8.2 for a sample constructivist lesson format.

Note that this style of expressing a lesson contains headings that require verbiage for content, grade level, unit title, lesson title, duration of the lesson, and length of class period, among other things. It also asks how the lesson meets Common Core and State Standards and it asks for information about adaptations. Certainly, there are many ways to write lesson plans and some of you may be in school districts that require a specific format. We acknowledge the diversity of formats and we are not pushing one format for writing out a lesson plan.

Having been K–12 teachers, we recognize that meticulously filling in each box on a lesson plan may feel onerous. We hardly have time to eat lunch most days. But taking time to think through your lessons, to carefully plan the beginning, middle, and end of each lesson, will enable you to not only create great experiences for students, but also to become more confident with time management, transitions between activities, and knowing how to move students toward the learning aims. Once you begin to feel proficient in designing and implementing various forms, you may find yourself using shorthand for some of your lesson plans. Some of us lesson plan on a desk calendar, some of us use note cards, some of us use Google Docs. In this text we have used a two-column format to make visible what teachers are thinking and what students will do. Now we also suggest that the format we have used may be a useful tool for you. That is, for those of you not required to follow a particular format, consider the format we have used throughout—and feel free to embellish with your own additions that you will find relevant when you revisit the lesson later on.

UNIT PLANNING

In this book we focused on lesson planning, which we note covers both short and long periods of time. That is, a lesson plan could refer to a

Figure 8.2. Detailed EEL DR C Lesson Template

Teacher Name:	
Content & Grade Level:	
Unit Title:	
Lesson Title:	
Day of Lesson:	
Duration of Lesson:	
Length of Class Period:	
Common Core / State Standards:	
Measurable Lesson Objectives:	
Materials and Resources Needed:	
Anticipatory Set:	*Enroll:*
Procedures and Research-Based Instructional Approaches:	*Experience:* *Label:* *Demonstrate:*
Differentiation:	
Lesson Closure and Wrap-up:	*Review:* *Celebrate:*
Adaptations for Students with Exceptionalities:	

half-hour or hour lesson or it could refer to a set of activities that may take a few days. We have not, however, covered how one might sequence lesson plans to build a unit. Excellent resources for this are available; we like *Understanding by Design* (UbD) by Wiggins and McTighe, as well as online sources like EduTopia.org. We have found it is helpful to think through the unit planning process first to see the bigger picture of a 2-to-6-week unit plan before working our way down to the detailed, minute-by-minute nature of a daily lesson plan. To give you a clearer sense of what that might look like, we offer a brief overview of the process we teach our own students as they design units (see Figure 8.3).

Begin the unit planning process by selecting a unit of study in your content area that can last from 2 to 6 weeks. You may need to consult district curriculum guides, veteran teachers, standards, and other resources. Next, think about the really big ideas, not the small details, that you want your students to learn and experience in that unit; these should be meaningful ones that they will remember long after they have left your classroom. After developing that list, design summative and formative assessments that will help you evaluate whether your students have learned the content. Traditional assessments may include tests, quizzes, and diagrams; innovative assessments may include role-plays, artistic representations,

Figure 8.3. Unit Planning Process

1. Identify the content to be taught, which may be based upon district guides, department agreements, or other external sources like standards and textbooks. Determine the length of time you have available for the unit within your yearly scope.
2. Articulate overarching learning aims, big ideas, experiences, and outcomes for your students.
3. Design formative and summative assessments, whether traditional or innovative. Ensure the assessments address your learning aims and provide many opportunities and formats for students to demonstrate learning.
4. Create a calendar and sequence the learning logically—by skills and experiences that build upon each other toward the big ideas, outcomes, and learning aims you have identified.
5. Think about experiences you can and want to provide for students. Who are your students? How can you engage them in the inclusive learning environment?
6. Match ideas and skills to various lesson plan approaches and consider blending some together if desired. See if you can include at least two or three approaches in each unit.
7. Sketch out each lesson plan and then fill in the details as you are ready. You might want to create a binder, folder, or box for your unit plans.

and student-organized service projects. These assessments should provide students a variety of ways to show what they are learning. Thinking about formative and summative assessments together provides you with a way to consider multiple forms of representation, student-driven projects, and traditional tests or quizzes as appropriate. After articulating the big ideas, the variety of assessments, and your overarching learning aims, identify the content you will need to teach your students to be successful on the summative assessments. Then sequence that content in a logical way in a unit plan calendar.

Now that you have your general structure, think about what experiences you can and want to provide for students. Who are your students? How can you engage them in the inclusive learning environment? Keeping your students in mind (always keep your students in mind!), match ideas and skills to various lesson plan approaches and consider blending some together if desired. See if you can include at least two or three approaches in each unit, whether blended or used individually. While there are certainly many ways to plan units, this framework is a guide for you to plan with purpose.

UNIT PLANS USING A SINGLE APPROACH

Most often, unit plans are comprised of lesson plans that employ several of the approaches we have outlined in this text. We believe that doing so creates variety, allows teachers to be intentional about selecting models for specific lessons, and helps lessen the likelihood of monotony and boredom for students and teachers alike. Nonetheless, teachers may have a reason to plan a unit using a single approach for all of its lessons. That could well be the case in a school where social–emotional learning is adopted across the curriculum and teachers are asked to incorporate social–emotional learning. We reiterate: In a situation like that, you can blend the approaches. But for teachers who wish to write single-approach unit plans, we offer some suggestions for how you might go about that.

In the behavioral approach, determine how much content will need to be covered. Next, decide whether the content requires one, two, or three weeks, or longer. What concepts and skills must be covered? Writing out a list of all the behavioral objectives can help here. Design the summative assessments to match the behavioral objectives. After that, sequence activities in a logical order that scaffolds them up to the summative assessment(s), which manifests in a unit calendar of topics.

In the constructivist approach, teachers ought to stay focused on individual learning and meaning-making. For the EEL DR C model, you might utilize backward design, deciding first what outcomes ought to be achieved by students. Then create a sequence of activities that alternates between large- and small-group learning opportunities. Individual work may include answering questions, beginning homework, or taking a test or quiz, and these opportunities should be provided along the way to reach the overall outcomes desired.

In the aesthetic approach, we recommend beginning by planning out what needs to be learned over a given period of time. Perhaps the goal is to teach a social studies unit over a period of 3 weeks. Next, delineate on a calendar what activities will take place over the 3 weeks, aiming to create a rhythm of activities that oscillate between students taking in information and expressing themselves. Utilize CRISPA across the unit and not only within individual lesson plans. So, for example, the C of CRISPA needs to be brought in several times over a 3-week unit. It cannot be used once at the beginning and be forgotten. The teacher needs to make sure students connect and stay connected to the content. Within the 3-week unit, look for balance of the C, R, I, S, P, and A. Is imagination brought in week 1 but not utilized in weeks 2 and 3? Where is the risk-taking, and how often is it manifested? Every element of CRISPA does not need to be brought in each day or even over several days. But we would suggest that each element be brought in at least once over the 3 weeks, or at least once in any unit.

In the ecological approach, we noted that lesson plans do not necessarily follow a sequence that one may find in other approaches. Nonetheless, some guidelines were offered, and these same guidelines could be followed in creating a unit. Teachers may still begin by working with students collaboratively in designing investigative questions. Then an experience-based objective would be explored and created to account for the unit set of ideas and activities. Design activities to include caring, interconnectedness, and integrity over a longer stretch of time. As the last step, leave time for the students to decide and take action. Note that this last activity may take a week in itself.

Finally, an integrated social–emotional learning approach would also use and broaden the sequencing ideas found in the lesson plans. The overall structure of the unit will include inclusion activities introducing both academic and social–emotional content to be covered in the unit, a body of ideas and skills focused on engaging practices, and time at the end of the unit focusing on reflection. Across the unit, make sure that the competencies of self-awareness, self-management, social awareness, relationship skills, and responsible decisionmaking are included. These competencies could be created by students jointly with teachers.

The inclusion activities at the beginning of the unit ought to invite students to explore their interpersonal skills as related to content. Such activities could take place over a series of days. In short, the activities should establish, nurture, and grow an inclusive classroom environment. The body of the ISEL lessons ought to cover at least one engaging practice that promotes SEL (e.g., pair-share, jigsaw, Socratic Seminar, etc.). Depending on the length of the unit, several engaging practices may be utilized. As noted earlier, activities should promote high engagement, collaboration, moments for creating, evaluating, reflecting, and sharing, and each of these could be done over a series of days, thus creating a unit that takes place over a week or two. Finally, the optimistic closure provides time for reflection. Such activities could also span a few days and take place at the end of the unit.

BRINGING IT ALL TOGETHER

Throughout this text, we have been intentional in sharing that we have been K–12 classroom teachers and have worked with pre- and inservice teachers in writing and implementing curriculum. We have done this to illustrate that we have experienced, firsthand, that the ideas expressed in this book can make a classroom come alive. We have been in professional development workshops where teachers have cried because they remembered how life-giving curriculum writing can be. We have seen students who are normally reserved or detached become engaged and enlivened when teachers implement some of these models. In short, these lesson plan approaches aren't just interesting theoretical ideas; they are transformative when put into practice.

Planning with purpose and teaching perceptively leads to classrooms that are vibrant, intellectually challenging, and fun. These classrooms are well managed because the teacher has built meaningful, caring relationships with students and provides relevant, engaging content. The idea of a quiet classroom being a well-managed classroom is not what planning with purpose and perceptive teaching are all about. In these classrooms students collaborate, think critically, create, vision, and make important connections. Students engage because they see relevance, they are supported, and they have some autonomy to make decisions, to make mistakes, and to grow. We argue strongly that if we want to reform schools, we need to enliven them by empowering teachers to be curriculum makers who invigorate and inspire their students. Planning with purpose allows you to do just that. Whether you are new to the teaching profession, are relatively early in your journey as a teacher, or you have been in a K–12 classroom for some time, applying the ideas from this book can transform your classroom and your career.

In our careers, we have read countless curriculum texts claiming to be the next big thing. We have seen the proverbial pendulum in education swing back and forth from one new curriculum to the next or from one set of standards to another new and improved set. We have been to countless professional development sessions that will "transform your classroom." The ideas in this text are not any of those things. These ideas are realistic, easily applicable, and can aid you in providing a remarkable educational experience for your students. We invite you to take the leap of faith and apply these ideas in your teaching. They *will* help you be the transformative teacher you always hoped to be.

Behaviorist Lesson Plan Template and Examples

Behaviorist Lesson Plan Template

TOPIC

Teacher Thinking . . .	Students and Teacher Doing . . .
Lesson Plan Element: Anticipatory Set	
How will I get students' attention and focus their learning?	
Objective and Purpose	
State the ABCD learning objective(s) and the purpose for learning. How many do I need?	
Input/Direct Instruction	
What kind of information must I provide so students can meet the objective?	
Modeling (I Do)	
What ways might I show the students the process or skill? What errors and misunderstandings do I anticipate? How might I correct them?	
Checking for Understanding	
How will I monitor their progress? Will this be informal or formal? Individual or whole group?	

(continued)

Behaviorist Lesson Plan Template *(continued)*

Teacher Thinking . . .	Students and Teacher Doing . . .
	Guided Practice (We Do)
What kinds of practice problems might I provide for the skills being taught? How can I organize them so they vary in complexity?	
	Independent Practice (You Do)
What kinds of work should students practice independently toward mastery? Will this be done in class or for homework?	
	Evaluation and Closure
What should I remind them of that we covered during the lesson? How will I do one last check for understanding?	

Notes:

Materials:

Time and Space:

Behaviorist Lesson Plan Example

3rd-Grade Language Arts: Reading

Teacher Thinking . . .	Students and Teacher Doing . . .
	Lesson Plan Element: Anticipatory Set
How will I get students' attention and focus their learning?	Students will become "reading detectives" as they listen for key details and character feelings during the story *Me and Uncle Romie* by Claire Hartfield. Afterward, students will play the game *Roll & Retell* to discuss the story in pairs or small groups.
	Objective and Purpose
State the ABCD learning objective(s) and the purpose for learning. How many do I need?	*North Carolina State Standards*: RL.3.1. Answer *who* and *what* questions to demonstrate understanding of details in a familiar text. RL.3.2 Associate details with events in stories from diverse cultures. RL.3.3 Identify the feeling of characters in a story. RL.3.5 Determine the beginning, middle, and end of a familiar story in order. *Lesson Objective*: Students will recount the story *Me and Uncle Romie* from beginning to end by citing key details, character feelings, and the central message. *Lesson Purpose*: By analyzing a text for key details and central ideas, students will be able to summarize a story.
	Input/Direct Instruction
What kind of information must I provide so that students can meet the objective?	This is the second time students will have heard the story. During the initial reading by the teacher, students were asked to "listen for pleasure." During this lesson, students will listen to an audio recording of *Me and Uncle Romie* and have their own copy of the story. Before the story, students will be instructed to mark an "ID" (important detail) or "CF" (character feeling) on a sticky note while listening to the story and place it on the corresponding book page while following along.

(continued)

Behaviorist Lesson Plan Example *(continued)*

Teacher Thinking . . .	Students and Teacher Doing . . .
	Modeling (I Do)
What ways might I show the students the process or skill? What errors and misunderstandings do I anticipate? How might I correct them?	While listening to the audio recording, the teacher will pause the story and note the first instance of an important detail and a character feeling. The teacher will model the "ID" and "CF" notation at each initial pause and how to place the sticky on the book page.
	Checking for Understanding
How will I monitor their progress? Will this be informal or formal? Individual or whole group?	While moving around the classroom during the story, the teacher will assist and informally monitor students to make sure they are following along and using the sticky notes correctly. Excessive use or lack of use of sticky notes may be anecdotally noted. However, the teacher will not correct usage unless absolutely necessary. Additionally, the teacher will pause the story occasionally to ask for student suggestions regarding what they just heard (ex.: "Why do you think I paused the story? Did you hear something that is an important detail or character feeling? What do we need to write on our sticky note? Where does it go?)
	Guided Practice (We Do)
What kinds of practice problems might I provide for the skills being taught? How can I organize them so they vary in complexity?	Students will play *Roll & Retell* in partner pairs or small groups. The pairs/groups will be determined beforehand to create a balance of academic and social levels to promote positive discussions and sharing. The teacher will model with students how to play *Roll & Retell* with dice and a "prompt poster" and discuss each of the six discussion prompts found on the poster: 1. *What do you think is the central message of the story?* 2. *How do the feelings of the characters change throughout the story?* 3. *What challenge, problem, or situation do the characters face in the story?* 4. *Where did the story take place, and is this important?* 5. *What were some of the major events in the story?* 6. *How did the characters resolve the problem, meet the challenge?*

Teacher Thinking . . .	Students and Teacher Doing . . .
	Students will use their books and sticky notes to help them recall and provide evidence to support their talking points while playing *Roll & Retell.* While moving around the classroom and meeting briefly with pairs/groups, the teacher will help prompt and guide discussions to focus students on important details. After playing *Roll & Retell*, students will gather in a circle on the rug to discuss some of their answers. The teacher will guide the discussion and prompt for deeper thinking when appropriate. The teacher will track ideas on chart paper for each of the different discussion prompts. The teacher will also ask students about their use of sticky notes and how they helped/didn't help.
Independent Practice (You Do)	
What kinds of work should students practice independently toward mastery? Will this be done in class or for homework?	After the group discussion, with the use of their book and sticky notes, students will complete a graphic organizer divided into *Beginning*, *Middle*, and *End* sections. The *Beginning* section will prompt students to note the characters introduced and the setting. The *Middle* section will have students note the situation/problem and the events that took place during the story. The *End* section will have students identify how the story concluded, what problems were solved, and the central message. Each section will have space for a small illustration in addition to their notes. At completion, students will turn in their work and transition to literacy centers. As an extension activity, students will use their graphic organizer to create a collage art piece (similar to Uncle Romie's art from the story and illustrations from the book). Students will select or create an item to add to the collage representative of each section of the story, character feelings, and important details. Students will later use their art piece to retell the story *Me and Uncle Romie* citing specific details, events, feelings, and central message.
Evaluation and Closure	
What should I remind them of that we covered during the lesson? How will I do one last check for understanding?	On a 4×6 note card, students will list three key details, events, or feelings from the story. They will share with a partner and then turn in to the teacher before transitioning to the next lesson.

(continued)

Behaviorist Lesson Plan Example *(continued)*

Notes: Make sure to look for other literacy-based opportunities such as writing prompts related to the text, higher-level vocabulary, and additional art-related connections.

Materials: Roll & Retell prompt poster (multiple copies or slide), dice, multiple copies of *Me and Uncle Romie*, audio recording of *Me and Uncle Romie*, graphic organizer, sticky notes, chart paper, markers, pencils, mix of art materials for collage activity, 4×6 note cards

Time and Space: 45–60 minutes, classroom

Behaviorist Lesson Plan Example

Grade 7, Currency and Unit Rates

Teacher Thinking . . .	Students and Teacher Doing . . .
Lesson Plan Element: Anticipatory Set	
How will I get students' attention and focus their learning?	Students will create their own paper currency. Students will design the front and back of a paper currency, create a name for their currency, and design a symbol to represent their currency.
Objective and Purpose	
State the ABCD learning objective(s) and the purpose for learning. How many do I need?	CCSS.MATH.CONTENT.7.RP.A.1 Students will compute unit rates associated with ratios of fractions, including ratios of lengths, areas, and other quantities measured in like or different units. www.corestandards.org/Math/Content/7/RP/ Lesson Objective: Students will apply their knowledge of computing unit rates by accurately computing the unit cost of their own currency in comparison to the currencies created by their classmates. Purpose: Students will practice computing unit cost. Students will be provided a real-world experience that supports their understanding of the importance of unit cost in our global economy and their personal lives.
Input/direct instruction	
What kind of information must I provide so students can meet the objective?	Students will receive a review of unit rate as the teacher demonstrates how to calculate the unit rate of two different measurements such as inches and feet. Students will be provided with the definition of unit cost. Students will watch as the teacher demonstrates how to calculate the unit cost between two different currencies such as dollars and pesos. Students will discuss how unit rate and unit cost are similar and different with a partner and then whole class.

Teacher Thinking . . .	Students and Teacher Doing . . .
	Modeling (I Do)
What ways might I show the students the process or skill? What errors and misunderstandings do I anticipate? How might I correct them?	Students will follow along as the teacher models how to compute the unit cost of different currencies in comparison to the U.S. dollar. Students will be provided common errors of unit cost such as placing the incorrect currency in the denominator of the fraction ratio. As a class, students will create a rule to avoid this common mistake.
	Checking for Understanding
How will I monitor their progress? Will this be informal or formal? Individual or whole group?	Students will complete guided practice problems using miniature whiteboards and erasable markers at their desk. Students will hold up their whiteboards for the teacher to check their understanding.
	Guided Practice (We Do)
What kinds of practice problems might I provide for the skills being taught? How can I organize them so they vary in complexity?	Students will select a good or service they must set a price for with their currencies such as a movie ticket or a car wash. This should be a good or service the students understand the value of. Students will provide their teacher with the value for the good or service in their currency as she records it in a chart. Students will practice computing the unit cost between the currencies of several students. Students will share their answers with the teacher by holding up their whiteboards.
	Independent Practice (You Do)
What kinds of work should students practice independently toward mastery? Will this be done in class or for homework?	Students will select 10 currencies created by their classmates for which they would like to compute the unit cost with their own currency. Students will record their work by hand in a graphic organizer. Students will calculate the unit cost with 100% accuracy as they will be able to use a calculator to double-check their work. If a student finds they have made a computation error, they must revise their math computations on their graphic organizer to fix their error. Students will begin this independent practice in class and will complete the graphic organizer for homework.

(continued)

Behaviorist Lesson Plan Example *(continued)*

Teacher Thinking . . .	Students and Teacher Doing . . .
	Evaluation and Closure
What should I remind them of that we covered during the lesson? How will I do one last check for understanding? How will I evaluate student learning of the established objective?	Students will complete an exit ticket with three unit cost problems to demonstrate their knowledge of the objective and their ability to transfer their knowledge of unit cost to new math problems.

Notes: May give students time to share with each other or with families for homework

Materials: Paper and markers/pencils, scissors to create currency, guided practice problems, miniature whiteboards, erasable markers, calculators, graphic organizers

Time and Space: 45 minutes; classroom or library

Behaviorist Lesson Plan Example

High School, Social Studies: Single-Day Lesson, Political Perspectives and Impact on Policy

Teacher Thinking . . .	Students and Teacher Doing . . .
	Lesson Plan Element: Anticipatory Set
How will I get students' attention and focus their learning?	The teacher will post a word/phrase on the board that represents a controversial topic (such as gun control, health care, or immigration). The students will give their opinions about the topic.
	Objective and Purpose
State the ABCD learning objective(s) and the purpose for learning. How many do I need?	***Colorado Academic Standard***: The students will be able to identify how policy proposals and decisions of elected representatives reflect specific ideals, values, and beliefs that are often affiliated with a political party. (SS09-GR.HS-S.4-GLE.3- EO.e) ***Lesson Objective***: Students will apply their knowledge of the ideals, values, and beliefs common to the Democratic or Republican political parties with greater than 85% accuracy as related to a proposed policy.
	Input/Direct Instruction
What kind of information must I provide so that students can meet the objective?	The teacher will describe how the contemporary political positions of the Democratic and Republican parties provide the foundation for policy decisions. The students will capture two column notes representing the ideals, values, and beliefs that are often affiliated with the Democratic and Republican political parties.

Teacher Thinking . . .	Students and Teacher Doing . . .
	Modeling (I Do)
What ways might I show the students the process or skill? What errors and misunderstandings do I anticipate? How might I correct them?	The teacher will choose a primary or secondary source representing a U.S. policy to illustrate the ideals, values, and beliefs of the proposing political party that are represented within the policy.
	Checking for Understanding
How will I monitor their progress? Will this be informal or formal? Individual or whole group?	The teacher will post signs on each side of the room (Democrat and Republican). The teacher will then read statements from additional policies and have students choose the side of the room they believe represents the ideals, values, and/or beliefs of the proposing political party.
	Guided Practice (We Do)
What kinds of practice problems might I provide for the skills being taught? How can I organize them so they vary in complexity?	The teacher will provide primary and secondary source documents that reflect contemporary political positions of the Democratic and Republican parties (on issues such as health care, gun control, immigration, etc.) Students will choose one document and will identify how the ideals, values, and/or beliefs of the proposing political party influence the proposition.
	Independent Practice (You Do)
What kinds of work should students practice independently toward mastery? Will this be done in class or for homework?	Students will create a policy proposal in written form, for a controversial topic of their choice, that is representative of the ideals, values, and beliefs often affiliated with the Democratic or Republican political party. The students must cite three pieces of textual evidence from a primary or secondary source in their rationale. The proposal should be written in narrative format.
	Evaluation and Closure
What should I remind them of that we covered during the lesson?	Review with students the requirements for the policy proposal and take questions. Ask them to watch for these topics in news sources. On a short exit ticket, ask students to write their topic and the opposing main arguments.

Materials: Primary and secondary source documents (or computer) reflecting policies influenced by contemporary political positions. Computers or paper to capture proposal in narrative form.

Time and Space: 60–90 minutes; classroom space with room to move for *Checking for Understanding* activity

Constructivist Lesson Plan Template and Examples

Constructivist Lesson Plan Template

TOPIC

Teacher Thinking . . .	Students and Teacher Doing . . .
Lesson Plan Element: Enroll	
How will I hook the students to provide an entrée into a deeper experience with the content?	
Experience	
What kind of experience can I create for students to have an initial exploration with the content?	
Label	
I have to make sure I tell them what they just did. Also, what kind of information must I provide in a minilesson so that students can illustrate understanding of the concept I'm teaching? Emergent Understandings: How are we focused on individualized meaning-making?	
Demonstrate	
What ways might students illustrate understanding of the concept I'm trying to teach? What kinds of spaces can I create for students to grapple with the content?	
Review	
How can I formatively assess that students met the learning targets while getting them to capture their thinking?	

Teacher Thinking . . .	Students and Teacher Doing . . .
Celebrate	
How can I wrap up the lesson and celebrate their learning?	

Notes:
Materials:
Time and Space:

Constructivist Lesson Plan Example

4th- and 5th-Grade Physical Education: Perseverance and Teamwork

Teacher Thinking . . .	Students and Teacher Doing . . .
Lesson Plan Element: Enroll	
How will I hook the students to provide an entrée into a deeper experience with the content?	At the end of the last class period, the teacher spoke briefly about *Adventure Challenge* and what is required to be successful (perseverance & teamwork). Students briefly brainstormed their own ideas and shared out. When students first enter the gym, the obstacles and equipment are already set up to spark student interest, engagement, and motivation. Before assigning teams, the teacher opens the discussion to students to address what strategies they will use to ensure success with their team. Ideas are tracked on chart paper by the teacher.
Experience	
What kind of experience can I create for students to have an initial exploration with the content?	During the class period, the teacher briefly introduces a cooperative game; give students 2–3 minutes to strategize and practice with the equipment before they start. Each game is not meant to last very long (5–10 minutes) so a variety of games can be played. At the end of each cooperative game experience, students meet with the teacher to briefly discuss several strategies that helped their team be successful, and strategies that did not work so well. Ideas are tracked on the chart paper.
Label	
I have to make sure I tell them what they just did. Also, what kind of information must I provide in a minilesson so that students can illustrate understanding of the concept I'm teaching?	The teacher highlights elements of teamwork and perseverance (emergent understanding) that are demonstrated during each game to prompt even more positive interactions during the next game. The cooperative games for this class period are: *The Shapes of Us, A Bridge to Somewhere, Blind Battle Bots, Capture the Beanbag,* and *Crossing the River.*

(continued)

Constructivist Lesson Plan Example *(continued)*

Teacher Thinking . . .	Students and Teacher Doing . . .
	Label (continued)
Emergent Understandings: How are we focused on individualized meaning-making?	*Adventure Challenge* will stretch over several class periods and the teacher will routinely conduct discussion-oriented minilessons at the beginning of each class highlighting positive and negative attributes for cooperative success. The teacher guides the discussion highlighting problem solving and critical thinking (perseverance) and constructive communication and compromise (teamwork).
	Demonstrate
What ways might students illustrate understanding of the concept I'm trying to teach? What kinds of spaces can I create for students to grapple with the content?	Students demonstrate understanding by exhibiting positive communication within their team that successfully leads to productive problem solving and cooperation. In a variety of cooperative games, students have a mix of opportunities to think critically and communicate with others for mutual success.
	Review
How can I formatively assess that students met the learning targets while getting them to capture their thinking?	The teacher takes anecdotal notes while moving around the obstacle course stations taking note of communication, frustration, risk-taking, critical thinking, problem solving, and overall participation. Additionally, the teacher reflects on the responses received on the chart paper before, during, and after the games. This will help inform future minilesson instruction and discussions.
	Celebrate
How can I wrap up the lesson and celebrate their learning?	Before the end of class, students meet as a whole group with the teacher to share their celebrations and successes during the games. Students and teacher also look back at their shared ideas on the chart paper. The teacher announces that *Adventure Challenge* will continue next class period with some of the same games and some that are new. The teacher asks, "What strategies will you bring to *Adventure Challenge* next time?"

Notes: There are several websites, including fitkidshealthykids.ca, where you can review the games beforehand.

Materials: Cooperative games and rules, game/obstacle course equipment (e.g., cones, mats, balls, beanbags, blindfolds, ropes, shuttlecocks), chart paper, markers

Time and Space: 45–60 minutes, gym or outdoor field

Constructivist Lesson Plan Example

Middle School Science Multi-Day Lesson, Systems of the Body

Teacher Thinking . . .	Students and Teacher Doing . . .
	Lesson Plan Element: Enroll
How will I hook the students to provide an entrée into a deeper experience with the content?	Students engage in a fast-paced game of *Simon Says* that includes running in place, jumping jacks, and other motor activities with limited opportunities to freeze. *The key is "fast-paced," so that students feel themselves breathing faster.*
	Experience
What kind of experience can I create for students to have an initial exploration with the content?	When the game is done, students capture on a piece of paper everything they feel and all the different ways their body was involved in the activity. The teacher prompts student thinking through questions, such as: "Were you breathing hard?" "Did you start to sweat?" "Were you nervous you were going to mess up?" After independent think time, students share in their table groups and then with the whole class. As a table group, students create a "Day in the Life of a Middle Schooler." The description must include at least one physical response and one emotional or chemical response by the body (e.g., hunger pains, feeling anxious, running at sports practice).
	Label
I have to make sure I tell them what they just did. Also, what kind of information must I provide in a minilesson so that students can illustrate understanding of the concept I'm teaching? Emergent Understandings: How are we focused on individualized meaning-making?	Tell the students, "You just explored the various systems in our bodies and how we use them in everyday activities. Throughout this unit, we will explore the various systems in our bodies, their importance, and how they may work together." Provide a brief minilesson on the major systems of the body (such as muscular, circulatory, skeletal, nervous, etc.). Define each system and explain its purpose. The students capture notes in their own notebook for each of the systems. Check the students' understanding by giving a function and having them write down the system on a personal whiteboard to hold up.

(continued)

Constructivist Lesson Plan Example *(continued)*

Teacher Thinking . . .	Students and Teacher Doing . . .
	Demonstrate
What ways might students illustrate understanding of the concept I'm trying to teach? What kinds of spaces can I create for students to grapple with the content?	Tell the students that they are going to have the opportunity to work in groups to identify the many ways that teenagers rely on their systems. After reviewing their "Day in Life of a Middle Schooler" creation, each group must identify a problem (such as stress, peer conflict, etc.), choose a system (or systems) that is impacted, and identify strategies for overcoming the impact. Students also identify additional systems that may be used as a part of the strategy. An example would be identifying our heart as a part of the circulatory system. A challenge would be that our heart rate may go up when we are stressed or angry. The students would then identify the complications of having a high heart rate and strategies for lowering their heart rate in those moments. The students can use computers, textbooks, videos, or reference pages to find their information. Sources must be cited. The students create a poster presentation to be shared with classmates during a gallery walk at a later date. The poster must highlight the problem, the system, and the strategies.
	Review
How can I formatively assess that students met the learning targets while getting them to capture their thinking?	On an exit ticket each day, students will respond to the prompt: *The system most impacted in my body today is . . .* *I know this because . . .*
	Celebrate
How can I wrap up the lesson and celebrate their learning?	Mid-lesson: Call out one positive noticing from each group and let students know you are excited to see their finished products that are being prepared for the gallery walk. End of lesson: Allow one student for each poster to share out an "Aha!" or new learning from the gallery walk. Students should share out for a poster not their own.

Notes: Consider inviting another class to view posters.

Materials: Posters, tape, whiteboards, dry erase markers, supplies to be creative, and computers, textbooks, videos, or reference pages for research

Time and Space: 2–3 class periods, depending on work production of students; space to work in groups

Constructivist Lesson Plan Example

High School Geometry, Representing Geometric Theorems

Teacher Thinking . . .	Students and Teacher Doing . . .
	Lesson Plan Element: Enroll
How will I hook the students to provide an entrée into a deeper experience with the content?	Show students a photograph of railroad tracks disappearing into the horizon. This picture must show straight railroad tracks with no curves. Provide students with a couple minutes to study the image.
	Experience
What kind of experience can I create for students to have an initial exploration with the content?	Prompt student discussion around the image encouraging questions and comments. Have pairs of students create a list of questions about the railroad tracks. Questions might include: Will the tracks go on forever? Will the tracks ever touch? Are the railroad ties between the tracks the same distance apart? Are the tracks straight or curved? Create a two-column chart on the board, the first column reading "Questions" and the second column reading "Answers." Have students share the questions they created with their partner and record them in the question column. Students analyze the photograph as they answer the questions they have created. Guide a class discussion to fill in the answer section of the two-column chart. Students may determine that the railroad tracks most likely won't go on forever. And that, while the railroad tracks shown in the picture are straight, not all railroad tracks are straight. They may state that the railroad ties must be the same length in order to keep the tracks the same distance from each other and prevent the train from derailing.
	Label
I have to make sure I tell them what they just did. Also, what kind of information must I provide in a minilesson so that students can illustrate understanding of the concept I'm teaching?	Ask students if they are able to identify the geometric theorem they have described by answering the questions about the picture of the railroad tracks. The students should be able to identify that the railroad tracks represent parallel lines or parallel segments. Ask the students if the railroad tracks are parallel lines or parallel segments. Have them explain the difference between the two.

(continued)

Constructivist Lesson Plan Example *(continued)*

Teacher Thinking . . .	Students and Teacher Doing . . .
	Label (continued)
Emergent Understandings: How are we focused on individualized meaning-making?	Tell the students that they have just created their own definition for parallel segments. As a class, formalize this definition for parallel segments based on their exploration of the photograph of railroad tracks. Record the student definition next to the photograph of the railroad tracks. Ask students how they can represent other geometric theorems with pictures of objects or people around them. Record their examples on the board.
	Demonstrate
What ways might students illustrate understanding of the concept I'm trying to teach? What kinds of spaces can I create for students to grapple with the content?	Tell students that they are going on a field trip around their school campus. They will walk around campus looking for representations of the geometric theorems they have been studying in class. Provide students with equipment to take photographs (school cameras, iPads, student cell phones, if allowed by school administrators). Provide students with a list of the geometric theorems they have learned to take with them on their walk. With students, walk outside around the school campus allowing them to see the geometric theorems in everyday objects. Encourage students to look at their surroundings with open eyes instead of having a specific theorem in mind that they would like to find and represent with a picture. After all the students have taken at least one picture, return to class. Instruct students to select one image they would like to use to represent a geometric theorem. Have students write a definition for the theorem in their own words and explain how the photograph they have taken represents the theorem they have defined.
	Review
How can I formatively assess that students met the learning targets while getting them to capture their thinking?	For homework, have students finish their theorem definition as well as their descriptive analysis of their photograph as a representation of that theorem. Determine whether the students were successful in visually demonstrating a geometric theorem, providing an accurate definition of that theorem, and providing an accurate analysis of how their photograph represented the theorem they defined.

Teacher Thinking . . .	Students and Teacher Doing . . .
Celebrate	
How can I wrap up the lesson and celebrate their learning?	Share with the students an appreciation for their hard work in visually representing geometric theorems. Inform students that we will be using one of the bulletin boards or walls in the classroom to create a wall gallery of their photographs. Let students know they will have the opportunity to conferencc with the teacher to edit their artwork caption (the theorem definition and descriptive analysis) before it is mounted on the wall. Their representations of geometric theorems will be hung on the wall for students and teachers to admire and learn from.

Notes: Be sure to pair students with people they normally do not work with. Let the principal know that we will be exploring campus for part of the lesson.

Materials: Photo of railroad tracks, devices to take pictures, and list of geometric theorems students have learned

Time and Space: This lesson should take about 120 minutes. This lesson takes place in the classroom, around the school campus, and at students' homes.

Aesthetic Lesson Plan Template and Examples

Aesthetic Lesson Plan Template

TOPIC

Teacher Thinking . . .	Students and Teacher Doing . . .
Lesson Plan Element: Creating the Expressive Objective	
What am I going to teach that is in the curriculum? How can students have a wow experience with the content?	
Designing the Experience from the Inside Out: Connections	
Looking at the four types of connections, in what ways can I help the students make meaningful connections to the content? *Intellectual*: Some students will connect to the ideas right away. My task is to keep them engaged. *Social*: Some students will connect to the content through social interactions. *Sensorial*: Some students will connect to the content through any or all of their five senses. *Personal*: Some students will connect to the content through personal connections to time, culture, place, or people.	
Building Out the Experience by Looking at the CRISPA Menu	
What else can I do to help students realize the expressive objective? Consider risk-taking, imagination, sensory experience, perceptivity, and active engagement.	

Teacher Thinking . . .	Students and Teacher Doing . . .
Sequencing the Events	
How will I open the lesson? (Beginning) What is the order of experiences? (Middle) How will I critique the students' experience? (End)	

Notes:

Materials:

Time and Space:

Adornments (quotations, photos, sketches, and other interesting inspirations):

Aesthetic Lesson Plan Example

2nd-Grade Science: Interdependent Relationships in Ecosystems

Teacher Thinking . . .	Students and Teacher Doing . . .
Lesson Plan Element: Creating the Expressive Objective	
What am I going to teach that is in the curriculum?	Students learn about interdependent relationships in ecosystems by exploring the relationship between plants and seed distributing/pollinating animals.
How can students have a wow experience with the content?	The classroom library, *Sensory Station*, and overall classroom are outfitted with books and artifacts to prompt curiosity and exploration. The teacher has made an effort to create topic-related connections wherever they can be naturally made within the classroom (e.g., insect counters in the Math Center, science vocabulary on the Word Wall, poem of the week, flower display). Expressive objective: Students use their imagination and ingenuity to create an individual model of a seed dispersing and/or pollinating animal. Science Standards for Alaska: 2-LS2-2 Develop a simple model that mimics the function of an animal in dispersing seeds or pollinating plants. 2-LS4-1 Make observations of plants and animals to compare the diversity of life in different habitats.

(continued)

Aesthetic Lesson Plan Example *(continued)*

Teacher Thinking . . .	Students and Teacher Doing . . .
Designing the Experience from the Inside Out: Connections	
Looking at the four types of connections, in what ways can I help students make meaningful connections to the content? *Intellectual*: Some students will connect to the ideas right away. My task is to keep them engaged. *Social*: Some students will connect to the content through social interactions. *Sensorial*: Some students will connect to the content through any or all of their five senses. *Personal*: Some students will connect to the content through personal connections to time, culture, place, or people.	*Intellectual*: Before this lesson, the teacher will have read several books related to pollination and seed distribution during read-alouds throughout the week (e.g., *Flowers Are Calling* by Rita Gray). These books are also highlighted in the classroom library. Flower- and insect-trimmed stationary are available in the Writing Center. To start this lesson, the teacher asks students about the books they have been reading recently in class and how the various texts might be related (e.g., bees like flowers, seeds make flowers) followed by several brief *National Geographic* videos on the topic (5–10 minutes). *Social*: Through brief teacher-facilitated discussions throughout the lesson, students share their ideas (validation) and reflect on the ideas shared by others (positive constructive feedback). Additionally, students collaborate and discuss with teacher prompting and feedback during interactions in the *Sensory Station* and classroom library during Explore Time centers. *Sensorial*: Students visit the *Sensory Station* in the classroom. During the length of this unit, the station contains a variety of materials and tools for sensory exploration (e.g., magnifying glasses, pictures and models of flowers, plants, insects, seeds, fur samples, feathers, cotton balls, fuzzy pom-poms, clay, tongs/tweezers). In addition, the artistic process of animal model creation will engage a number of senses and sensory experiences. *Personal*: During read-alouds and discussions following the educational videos, students share personal experiences (e.g., I was stung by a bee, we plant flowers at home). In addition, for the culminating project, students create an individualized animal that mimics seed distribution and/or pollination.
Building Out the Experience by Looking at the CRISPA Menu	
What else can I do to help students realize the expressive objective? Consider risk-taking, imagination, sensory experience, perceptivity, and active engagement.	The teacher reviews the various traits (similarities/differences) of seed distributing and pollinating animals with students. After discussing the various craft resources and tools, students have access to the activity (e.g., glue, pipe cleaners, craft sticks, scissors, clay, feathers), and begin the planning process for their animals.

Teacher Thinking . . .	Students and Teacher Doing . . .
	Risk-taking, Imagination, & Active Engagement: Given the resources presented, students not only take risks as they sketch out and design their animals, but also when asked to present their animals upon completion. The teacher emphasizes creativity ("use your imagination") and details ("looking at it like a scientist") while still maintaining a viable way for the animals to pollinate and/or distribute seeds. After planning, students begin construction of their animals. This timeline will vary for individual students and potentially stretch over several days. The teacher should emphasize that students take their time and produce something they are proud to display (upcoming classroom museum/zoo). *Sensory Experience, Perceptivity, & Active Engagement*: Students are actively engaged in listening, viewing, and discussing while exploring types of seed distributing and pollinating animals and their relationships to plant life (e.g., videos, books, artifacts). *Sensory Station* experiences with tools and artifacts related to the topic and impromptu station discussions and conversations at recess and morning circle time ought to promote further curiosity and self-initiated investigations. The Sensory Station should include items for students to see, touch, smell, hear, and when appropriate, taste (e.g., pictures/ models, fur and feathers, audio of insect and bird noises, honey). Students also enter their notes, illustrations, and reflections regarding the unit in their *Science Journals*. This may take multiple journal entries.
Sequencing the Events	
How will I open the lesson? (Beginning) What is the order of experiences? (Middle)	*Beginning*: Students view educational videos and discuss interdependent relationships and seed distributing/pollinating animals. Exciting hook: "You get to create your own animal! What traits will your animal need?" *Middle*: (1) Discussion of necessary animal traits (tracked on whiteboard) related to videos and books on seed distributing or pollinating animals. (2) Introduction of craft materials and available tools. (3) Brief teacher modeling of the planning and production process and overall task expectations. (4) Students plan and produce their animals.

(continued)

Aesthetic Lesson Plan Example *(continued)*

Teacher Thinking . . .	Students and Teacher Doing . . .
Sequencing the Events (continued)	
How will I critique the students' experience? (End)	*End*: Students present to the class and display their animals in the classroom with corresponding notecards citing how the animal distributes seeds and/or pollinates. Toward the end of the unit, students record an entry in their *Science Journal* reflecting on their new understandings and unit experiences (notes, illustrations, photos).

Notes: This lesson is an opportunity for teachers to get students excited about science and creative at the same time. Make sure to look for inspiration in art, poetry, and the natural world to incorporate into the classroom and discussions.

Materials: Books and videos related to animal and plant interdependent relationships, craft materials for animal models, *Sensory Station* artifacts and exploration items, notecards, and animal/plant artwork

> *"If the bees disappear, we'll all be stung."—David Suzuki*
>
> *"The hum of bees is the voice of the garden."—Elizabeth Lawrence*

Time and Space: 45–60 minutes, classroom and outdoor areas (nature walk when possible)

Aesthetic Lesson Plan Example

9th-Grade Language Arts, Autobiographical Narrative

Teacher Thinking . . .	Students and Teacher Doing . . .
Lesson Plan Element: Creating the Expressive Objective	
What am I going to teach that is in the curriculum? How can students have a wow experience with the content?	Students practice their narrative skills by writing an autobiographical narrative. Individually, students select a leader or mentor whose life they would like to study. The selection can be an historical figure, a current leader, or an important figure in students' lives. Students write a letter as if they were that person narrating an event or experience to a friend, family member, or colleague of the historical figure they chose. Students gain insight and understanding of another person's world and life choices. The expressive objective of the lesson is for students to write with vivid imagery using their five senses to help readers connect to the experience they are narrating.
Designing the Experience from the Inside Out: Connections	
Looking at the four types of connections, in what ways can I help the students make meaningful connections to the content?	*Intellectual*: Students write a letter in autobiographical narrative form of a leader they are inspired by and/or personally connected to. Students are responsible for utilizing the narrative arc, correct grammar and syntax, and the structure of a formal letter.

Teacher Thinking . . .	Students and Teacher Doing . . .
Intellectual: Some students will connect to the ideas right away. My task is to keep them engaged. *Social*: Some students will connect to the content through social interactions. *Sensorial*: Some students will connect to the content through any or all of their five senses. *Personal*: Some students will connect to the content through personal connections to time, culture, place, or people.	*Social*: Students have the opportunity to share their autobiographical narratives in small-group reading sessions. *Sensorial*: Students create sentences or phrases with descriptive imagery that reference each of the five senses. *Personal*: Students have the freedom to select the subject of their written narratives and have the opportunity to choose an important event or experience from the subjects' lives.
Building Out the Experience by Looking at the CRISPA Menu	
What else can I do to help students realize the expressive objective? Consider risk-taking, imagination, sensory experience, perceptivity, and active engagement.	To support students in their descriptive imagery, they complete a five-column chart with the headers of each column reading sight, sound, taste, touch, and smell. Students write a sentence or phrase using descriptive imagery that connects to the event they have selected to write about. For example, one student may choose to write about Frida Kahlo as if they were her as a little girl sitting in her bedroom learning from the doctor that she has significant back trauma. They may imagine the sight of her small room in her house in Mexico. There may be sounds of adults speaking. There are tastes and smells of medication and a feeling of the weight of the blankets on her.
Sequencing the Events	
How will I open the lesson? (Beginning) What is the order of experiences? (Middle)	*Beginning*: To practice the skills of writing descriptive imagery, students complete a narrative description as a class with their teacher. Students describe their classroom using imagery and their five senses. *Middle*: 1. Students select a leader or mentor whose life they would like to study. This can be an historical figure, a current leader, or an important figure in students' lives. Students choose an event in their subject's life to narrate using the narrative arc. Students write their autobiographical narrative as a letter to a friend, family member, or colleague of the historical figure they chose. In the case of Frida Kahlo, for example, she may be writing to Diego Rivera.

(continued)

Aesthetic Lesson Plan Example *(continued)*

Teacher Thinking . . .	Students and Teacher Doing . . .
	Sequencing the Events (continued)
How will I critique the students' experience? (End)	2. To support students in focused research of their subject for their autobiographical narrative, students complete a brainstorming type of graphic organizer (a thinking map or web or fast write) to record descriptions. 3. Students complete their five-column descriptive imagery chart to identify and categorize the sensory details. Again, for example, students writing about Frida Kahlo may place the smell of medicine in the column labeled "smell." They might also place the sound of adults talking around her in the "sound" category. 4. Students write a draft of their autobiographical narrative letter including salutations, a recipient address, and sender address. Some students may choose to create a final draft that is representative of the time period. For example, they may use tea to stain the paper. Or they might use an actual typewriter. Or they could add scribbles or watercolor for the Kahlo example. *End*: Students engage in writing conferences with the teacher to discuss their: • utilization of the narrative arc • descriptive imagery capturing all five senses • syntax and grammar • letter structure Students edit their letters and share the final drafts of their autobiographical narratives in small-group reading sessions. In these reading sessions, students reflect and discuss their connections to their subjects as well as the process of writing an autobiographical narrative.

Notes: Perhaps begin by brainstorming historical figures from a variety of cultures.

Materials: Graphic organizer to explore descriptive imagery, devices to conduct research (computer, iPad, laptop), pencils

Time and Space: This lesson should take about 180 minutes, about three class periods, and needs to take place in an environment that supports student research on the Internet.

"Stories matter." —*Chimamanda Ngozi Adichie*

Aesthetic Lesson Plan Example

7th-Grade Math, Representing Fractions, Decimals, and Percents

Teacher Thinking . . .	Students and Teacher Doing . . .
Lesson Plan Element: Creating the Expressive Objective	
What am I going to teach that is in the curriculum? How can students have a wow experience with the content?	Students convert between fractions, decimals, and percents. Students represent parts of a whole in a hundreds chart (a 10 × 10 grid). The expressive objective is for students, through artistic representation of parts of a whole, to develop a deeper understanding of fractions, decimals, and percents. Students visually represent multiple ways to demonstrate parts of a whole.
Designing the Experience from the Inside Out: Connections	
Looking at the four types of connections, in what ways can I help the students make meaningful connections to the content? *Intellectual*: Some students will connect to the ideas right away. My task is to keep them engaged. *Social*: Some students will connect to the content through social interactions. *Sensorial*: Some students will connect to the content through any or all of their five senses. *Personal*: Some students will connect to the content through personal connections to time, culture, place, or people.	*Intellectual*: Students represent fractions, decimals, and percents by filling in a hundreds chart with colored pencils. *Social*: Students have the opportunity to partner share and peer edit. *Sensorial*: The students connect to the content through their sense of sight. Students apply elements of art (color and value) and principles of design to their images (balance and pattern). In this lesson plan the focus is on value and pattern. *Personal*: Students connect to the content through the personal choices they are able to make in their works of art.
Building Out the Experience by Looking at the CRISPA Menu	
What else can I do to help students realize the expressive objective? Consider risk-taking, imagination, sensory experience, perceptivity, and active engagement.	If possible, and motivated, students should review the elements of art and the principles of design to stimulate their background knowledge of these artistic tools. Place four large posters on the walls of the classroom. Label two posters "value" and the other two "pattern."

(continued)

Aesthetic Lesson Plan Example *(continued)*

<table>
<tr><th>Teacher Thinking . . .</th><th>Students and Teacher Doing . . .</th></tr>
<tr><td colspan="2">Building Out the Experience by Looking at the CRISPA Menu (continued)</td></tr>
<tr><td></td><td>Split students into groups of four and assign each group a poster. Have students rotate through the posters drawing or writing examples for each element and principle. For example, on the "value" poster, students could create a gradient scale by shading their pencil lightly and then darker across the paper. On the "pattern" poster, students could draw a circle, triangle, and square in a repeated pattern.
As a class, discuss and reflect upon the properties of each artistic tool.</td></tr>
<tr><td colspan="2">Sequencing the Events</td></tr>
<tr><td>How will I open the lesson? (Beginning)
What is the order of experiences? (Middle)
How will I critique the students' experience? (End)</td><td>Beginning: If motivated, students review the elements of art and the principles of design. Students discuss and provide examples of how the elements and principles are combined to create works of art. In this lesson, focus on value and pattern.
Middle: Students color an image on a 100-square grid. They must color the whole grid considering value and pattern. For example, they could make stripes, or squares within squares. They could also cut squares and make triangles. In this example, for "value," students could alternate dark, light, dark, light. Or they could do a gradient by starting out light at the top and getting darker as they get to the bottom of the grid.
Students record the ratio of each color they selected in comparison to the whole using reduced fractions, decimals, and percents. Students record their findings in a three-column chart, with the first column reading "Fraction," the second column reading "Decimal," and the third column reading "Percent." For example, a student may color 33 squares blue. In the fraction column they will write 33/100. In the decimal column they will write 0.33, and in the percent column they will write 33%. Note that in this example the fraction cannot be simplified.</td></tr>
</table>

Teacher Thinking . . .	Students and Teacher Doing . . .
	Next, on a second square grid, students create a second image using the same ratios of each color they used in the first design. For example, if 33% of the squares colored were blue in the first image, they must color 33 squares blue in the second image. Students must create a new pattern for their second image. For example, if students created a repeating pattern of vertical stripes in their first image, they might choose a horizontal pattern of repeating colors such as red, green, blue in their second image. In addition, students must use value in a new way. For example, if students used a horizontal gradient of light to dark across the grid in their first image, they may choose to do a vertical gradient of light to dark down their grid in the second image. *End*: After completing their two images in the hundreds grids, students pair-share, discussing and reflecting upon their use of pattern and value in their images. They check the accuracy of their partner's color ratios as recorded in their three-column chart. Students choose how they would like to display their artwork (class art portfolio, on a bulletin board, etc.).

Notes: In advance, review the elements of art and the principles of design (space, value, form, color, line, shape, texture, movement, etc.) to stimulate their background knowledge of these artistic tools.

Materials: Two "hundreds charts" per student, three-column chart (to record their fractions, decimals, and percents), coloring utensils (crayons, colored pencils, markers), scratch paper for conversions, calculators to accommodate students with learning challenges

Time and Space: This activity should take about 120 minutes and can be done in a variety of locations because so few materials are required. Students can work at their desk, in a flexible seating setting, or even outside.

> *"Mathematics is the art of giving the same name to different things." — Henri Poincaré*

Aesthetic Lesson Plan Example

Middle School, Social Studies, Multi-day Lesson, Exploring the 13 Colonies

Teacher Thinking . . .	Students and Teacher Doing . . .
Lesson Plan Element: Creating the Expressive Objective	
What am I going to teach that is in the curriculum? How can students have a wow experience with the content?	Students create sensory experiences for the social, geographic, and economic characteristics of the 13 colonies. Students create a montage and caption for one of the 13 colonies to present to the class.
Designing the Experience from the Inside Out: Connections	
Looking at the four types of connections, in what ways can I help the students make meaningful connections to the content? *Intellectual*: Some students will connect to the ideas right away. My task is to keep them engaged. *Social*: Some students will connect to the content through social interactions. *Sensorial*: Some students will connect to the content through any or all of their five senses. *Personal*: Some students will connect to the content through personal connections to time, culture, place, or people.	*Intellectual:* In a previous lesson, students learned about the 13 colonies. Students studied the social, geographic, and economic characteristics and what hardships the colonies faced. When creating the montage, students should consider the questions: What might it sound like if you were experiencing this picture? What might you smell? What would you see if you looked beyond the picture? *Social:* Students share with a partner a picture or item from their family that they believe reflects the characteristics of their family. Students also work in groups to create their montage projects. *Sensorial:* Students work in groups to use supplies and various items to create a montage of pictures that are representative of the characteristics and hardships of their colony. The supplies include items such as cotton, food, wood, sand, dirt, clothes, etc. Students should consider how the items relate to the sights, sounds, and smells representative of their colony. *Personal:* As a group, students take pictures of the artifacts chosen to represent the identity of the colony. Through creating the montage, students have the opportunity to connect with their colony at a deeper level.
Building Out the Experience by Looking at the CRISPA Menu	
What else can I do to help students realize the expressive objective? Consider risk-taking, imagination, sensory experience, perceptivity, and active engagement.	*Risk-Taking:* Students share a personal photo that represents their family identity. Opening up about their families can push middle school students outside of their comfort zone.

Teacher Thinking . . .	Students and Teacher Doing . . .
	Sensory Experience: Students consider the sights, sounds, and smells of each of the colonies as it relates to their individualized characteristics. Students explore many items for creating representations of their colony. Items can include food that is representative of the area, cotton balls, straw, toy animals to reflect the economy, or sand/dirt/grasses to reflect the geography. *Imagination:* Students tap into their imagination of what their colony may have been like during the time period. Students place items together that they feel reflect the social, geographic, and economic characteristics and take pictures to create a montage. *Active Engagement:* Students are actively engaged in identifying relevance for each of the colonies and working collaboratively to create their final products. *Perceptivity:* Students consider the subtleties between the colonies that created the different identities.
Sequencing the Events	
How will I open the lesson? (Beginning)	*Beginning:* Students begin by sharing their personal photos with partners. The warm-up activity includes three rounds, with partnerships changing after each round. The first round includes discussing the sights that are represented by their photo. For example, what was going on in their surroundings at the time the picture was taken? The second round includes the smells that may have been present at the time of the picture. For example, the smell of fresh air for a picture taken in the mountains. The third round includes the sounds that were present when the picture was taken. For example, the sound of laughter for a picture taken at a birthday party (risk-taking, connections, and active engagement).

(continued)

Aesthetic Lesson Plan Example *(continued)*

Teacher Thinking . . .	Students and Teacher Doing . . .
	Sequencing the Events (continued)
What is the order of experiences? (Middle) How will I critique the students' experience? (End)	*Middle:* The next activity requires students to split into 13 separate groups, each with their own colony. In each group, students work to discuss the identity of their colony and what items they believe can be put together to represent the social, geographic, and economic characteristics. Students need to consider the sensory experience they will be creating for their presentation and how they want their "audience" to feel when viewing their montage. The montage should evoke emotions around the positive characteristics of the colony, as well as the hardships (imagination). Students need to examine the various items and consider if they are the best representations of their colony (perceptivity). In addition, montages can include quotes that reflect their colony at that time. Montages can be created out of printed pictures that are put together for viewing or can insert pictures on a PowerPoint slide to be shared. *End*: Students conduct a quiet gallery walk, capturing their emotions and thoughts on a note catcher or piece of paper (*sensory*). The reflection should include perceived smells and sounds, as well as sights. After the gallery walk, students share out, as a class, their reflections and the differences they noticed about the colonies (*perceptivity*).

Notes: Consider inviting parents and community members in to participate in the gallery walk.

Materials: Sensory materials that represent the characteristics of the various colonies. Items can include cotton balls, straw, different types of food, plastic fish and animals, dirt, rocks, etc. Students will need either phones or computers to take pictures. If creating a printed montage, students need access to a printer and a way to post the pictures, as well as a computer to look up ideas and quotes, if needed.

Time and Space: 60–90 minutes and space for group work and the gallery walk.

> *"In photography there is a reality so subtle that it becomes more real than reality."*
> *—Alfred Stieglitz*

Ecological Lesson Plan Templates (Ecomindedness and Place-Based) and Examples

Ecomindedness Lesson Plan Template

TOPIC

Teacher Thinking . . .	Students and Teacher Doing . . .
Lesson Plan Element: Describe It (EBO)	
How can I describe the students' experience? Who, What, When, Where, Why, and How? Focus on the experience rather than the outcome. How will students demonstrate their understandings and developing beliefs through a multiplicity of outcomes?	
Locate It	
How can I help students find the content in its "natural" context? Where does this skill, idea, concept, or element of content reside? What examples can they find in their own lives, with their families, and their communities? *Interconnectedness*: Acknowledgment of the eclectic and complex relationships among all things; juxtaposition • How am I connected to the concepts and ideas? How is the content I am studying related to other concepts?	

(continued)

Ecomindedness Lesson Plan Template *(continued)*

Teacher Thinking . . .	Students and Teacher Doing . . .
Learn It	
How can I design an experience to help students explore and experience the concept where it is found? In what ways can I help students care about themselves, others near and far, human and non-human? How can I help students understand the usefulness and meaning of this concept for their lives? *Care*: Care for self; care for animals, plants and the earth; care for family, neighbors, and strangers and distant others • What does it mean to care about myself? How does caring for myself allow me to care for others? In what ways might I care for others near and far, human and non-human?	
Live It	
How can I help students think about their learning as a part of their construction of beliefs and values, along with decisionmaking? What values and beliefs are embedded in the lesson? How can I help students develop and act upon those values and beliefs? While some lessons may focus on immediate action, others may introduce a concept and generate many possibilities for living the ideas. For example, students might be introduced to thinking about habitat conservation, but the focus of the lesson is to help them connect their own habitat with animal habitats. *Integrity*: To act in accordance with one's beliefs; wholeness • How do I understand and develop my own beliefs and values related to content? What actions can I take, large and small, to act on my beliefs?	

Notes:

Materials:

Time and Place:

Place-Based Lesson Plan Template

TOPIC

Teacher Thinking . . .	Students and Teacher Doing . . .
Lesson Plan Element: Investigative Questions	
How might I design experiences collaboratively with students that honor their past and present experiences? Some examples: Where are we? Who lives here? How did our community form? Where does our food come from? Where do we get our drinking water? What migration patterns exist in our communities?	
Experience-Based Objective	
How can I describe the students' experience? Who, What, When, Where, Why, and How? Focus on the experience rather than the outcome. How will students demonstrate their understandings and developing beliefs through a multiplicity of outcomes?	
Direct Exploration of Places and Development of a Sense of Place	
What opportunities exist for students to explore a particular place? How can these experiences help them develop a sense of place?	
Multiple Pathways to Experience and Explore Ecomindedness, Including Caring, Interconnectedness, and Integrity (Optional)	
What are the pathways to experience and explore caring, interconnectedness, and integrity?	
Positive Action	
How can the students act to improve the situation being explored?	
Inter- or Multidisciplinary Explorations	
How might I bring in interdisciplinary learning?	

Notes:

Materials:

Time and Space:

Ecomindedness Lesson Plan Example

Kindergarten Math: Geometry

Teacher Thinking . . .	Students and Teacher Doing . . .
	Lesson Plan Element: Describe It (EBO)
How can I describe the students' experience? Who, What, When, Where, Why, and How? What standards or curriculum concepts do I need and want to address?	Students will become more connected to their environment and community by identifying, exploring, manipulating, and creating shapes. With a focus on triangles, the teacher additionally hopes to connect the concepts of *diversity* (different types of triangles, different types of people) and *cooperation* (shapes/people working together can create something new). This focus has two distinct purposes: academic—triangles that are not equilateral are routinely mislabeled at this age—and social—although we may have differences, we also have many similarities and can work together for the benefit of our community. *Who*: Students with the guidance of teachers and caregivers. *What*: Students will learn to identify shapes in isolated and real-world contexts, create shapes, and manipulate shapes to build new shapes. *When and where*: Students will explore shapes inside and outside of the classroom with shape models and real-world shape artifacts. Students will also be encouraged to explore shapes at home and in the community. *How*: Students will engage in a series of classroom and outdoor activities, exploration opportunities (*Math Center, Building Center, Art Center, Shape Walks*) and inquiry-based discussions. *Why*: Students will better understand how shapes relate to the physical and natural world around them and draw connections to physical and social contexts within the classroom and greater community. *Common Core State Standards*: CCSS.MATH.CONTENT.K.G.A.2 Correctly name shapes regardless of their orientations or overall size. CCSS.MATH.CONTENT.K.G.A.3 Identify shapes as two-dimensional or three-dimensional.

Teacher Thinking . . .	Students and Teacher Doing . . .
	CCSS.MATH.CONTENT.K.G.B.5 Model shapes in the world by building shapes from components and drawing shapes. CCSS.MATH.CONTENT.K.G.B.6 Compose simple shapes to form larger shapes.
	Locate It
How can I help students find the content in its "natural" context? Where does this skill, idea, concept, or element of content reside? What examples can they find in their own lives, with their families, and their communities? *Interconnectedness*: Acknowledgment of the eclectic and complex relationships among all things; juxtaposition • How am I connected to the concepts and ideas? How is the content I am studying related to other concepts?	In a circle on the rug, students will review each shape for this lesson (circle, square, triangle, rectangle, cube, sphere; *extension shapes*: cone, cylinder, hexagon) with teacher guidance. The teacher will present each tangible shape (2D cutouts and 3D models) and ask students to share their ideas. As each shape is identified, the teacher will present an additional picture or item of the shape represented in the *real world* (ex., triangle-shaped tree, square windows, sphere basketballs, Kandinsky painting) and ask for student input (ex., What do you know about shapes? Do you think shapes are important? Why? Where do you see shapes?). Students are invited to touch the shape models and trace/feel as they pass them around the circle ("1, 2, 3, that's enough for me" count and then pass; the teacher references a connection from the 3 count to the number of sides on a triangle through guided questioning). While students pass models around and/or view shapes, the teacher will ask students for examples of shapes *related* to their own lives. When necessary, the teacher will prompt students with ideas to spark connections (ex.: rectangle book, cube dice, circle hula hoop). Ideas will be tracked on the whiteboard with accompanying illustrations. If time permits, students will take turns drawing each of the 2D shapes on a partner's back. A quick culminating game of trying to "Guess the Shape" drawn by your partner is always fun!
	Learn It
How can I design an experience to help students explore and experience the concept where it is found?	Before students go to their table groups, the teacher will model drawing a triangle on the whiteboard and restate that triangles have three sides and three corners/angles.

(continued)

Ecomindedness Lesson Plan Example *(continued)*

Teacher Thinking . . .	Students and Teacher Doing . . .
	Learn It (continued)
In what ways can I help students care about themselves, others near and far, human and non-human? How can I help students understand the usefulness and meaning of this concept for their lives? *Care*: Care for self; care for animals, plants and the earth; care for family, neighbors, and strangers and distant others • What does it mean to care about myself? How does caring for myself allow me to care for others? In what ways might I care for others near and far, human and non-human?	Paper, pencils, and crayons will be distributed to each table group by student helpers. The teacher will prompt students to "draw a triangle and color it" (emphasis can be placed on "any size or color" if needed, but try to leave it open to student interpretation if possible, with minimal prompting). With an added twist, the teacher may prompt students to draw a face on their triangle similar to an emoji. This is meant to be a *Quick Draw* activity (5 minutes), so the teacher will give time reminders and countdown when it's time to wrap it up. After giving their triangle illustrations to the teacher, students are transitioned back to their circle seats around the rug. The teacher displays and shares each of the different student triangles with positive feedback drawing attention to unique differences and interesting similarities. Students are also invited to contribute their thoughts. The teacher will also show students a variety of triangle cutouts (ex.: right, isosceles, obtuse, acute) asking if they are triangles and discussing student responses with the group (ex., "Does it have three sides? What does that mean?"). The teacher will transition the discussion by asking students if they notice any similarities between triangles and people. The teacher may need to prompt this connection by citing how triangles can be different just like people can be different (ex., physical and social characteristics, but all still human beings just like all shapes with three sides are triangles). If students appear ready, the discussion may briefly transition to "Should we treat people that are different in a different way than people that are the same" and any other relevant and natural social conversations that may come up.

<table>
<tr><th>Teacher Thinking . . .</th><th>Students and Teacher Doing . . .</th></tr>
<tr><td colspan="2">Live It</td></tr>
<tr><td>How can I help students think about their learning as a part of their construction of beliefs and values, along with decisionmaking? What values and beliefs are embedded in the lesson?

How can I help students develop and act upon those values and beliefs?

While some lessons may focus on immediate action, others may introduce a concept and generate many possibilities for living the ideas. For example, students might be introduced to thinking about habitat conservation, but the focus of the lesson is to help them connect their own habitat with animal habitats.

Integrity: To act in accordance with one's beliefs; wholeness
• How do I understand and develop my own beliefs and values related to content?
What actions can I take, large and small, to act on my beliefs?</td><td>The teacher will transition students up from their seated position to a standing position in the circle, and give students a small baggie with each shape inside (cutouts for 2D and dice and marbles for 3D). The teacher will lead students in the Shape Hokey Pokey by calling out shapes prompting students to pull the corresponding shape out of their baggie and returning while singing and dancing for each shape (ex., You put your rectangle in, you put your rectangle out. You put your rectangle in and you shake it all about. You do the Hokey Pokey, and you turn yourself around. That's what it's all about!).

After several engaging rounds of the Hokey Pokey, the teacher will transition students into a line paired with their turn and talk partner and appropriate attire for going outside.

Students will gather with the teacher on the grass field outside. While in a circle, the teacher will give directions for pairs to "use their scientist eyes" and look for shapes all around the playground area and outdoor space. Student pairs will go on a Shape Walk and take turns tracking the shapes they see with illustrations and/or words with the use of blank paper, pens, and clipboards. The teacher will remind students of "good choices" and to listen for the whistle signal when it's time to gather again. Students will explore in pairs and document the shapes they see.

Students will transition back into the classroom and gather with partners on the rug. With teacher guidance, partner pairs will share some of the shapes they recorded. Students will share where they saw the shape in the real world and what they recorded. The teacher will also ask student pairs if they had different ideas/opinions when looking for shapes, or if their ideas happened to be the same. The teacher will highlight differences in student perspective to demonstrate how people may accomplish the same task but in a different way, and how individuals may see the same shape but with a different perspective.</td></tr>
</table>

(continued)

Ecomindedness Lesson Plan Example *(continued)*

Teacher Thinking . . .	Students and Teacher Doing . . .
	Live It (continued)
	The teacher will ask students to create an art piece utilizing the shapes that they have been discussing. The *Hokey Pokey* baggies will be distributed to students to aid them with their illustrations. The teacher may model how to draw shapes, but it's important not to over model to allow for more student creativity. In addition to the shape models and artifacts, the teacher may use Kandinsky paintings and other shape art to help inspire students. The teacher will emphasize that the illustration can be something real or from their imagination. If needed, this activity can be continued during future lessons or during center time. The teacher may also find it useful to reference *triangles* during future social discussions regarding differences and similarities, and conflict resolution.

Notes: Make sure to outfit classroom centers with shape books, manipulatives, posters, and displays (*Shape Museum*).

Materials: Plastic shape cutouts, wooden 3D blocks, pictures or slides (ex. buildings, moon) and tangible examples of *real-world* shapes (e.g., book, clock), whiteboard and markers, clipboards, pens, paper, crayons, markers, individual shape baggies (2D cutouts of each shape, marbles, dice)

Time and Space: 45–60 minutes, classroom and outdoor play area

Ecomindedness Lesson Plan Example

High School Art, Gentrification and Art

Teacher Thinking . . .	Students and Teacher Doing . . .
Lesson Plan Element: Experience-Based Objective	
How can I describe the students' experience? Who, What, When, Where, Why, and How? What standards or curriculum concepts do I need and want to address?	The students will explore and define gentrification and will seek to find examples within their own community. They will plan a field trip to explore how art intersects with gentrification while also speaking with community members about their experiences. Students will apply their knowledge of gentrification and make an artistic creation that reflects their viewpoint on their community. *Who:* Students with support from teacher and community contacts. *What:* Define gentrification. *When:* In class and on a sponsored field trip. *Where:* Local urban community experiencing gentrification. *Why:* To better understand the positive and negative consequences of gentrification and the place that art has within the context. *How:* Canvas and paint supplies Colorado Academic Standards—Visual Arts *Observe and Learn to Comprehend* Historical and cultural context are found in visual art (VA09-GR.HS-S.1-GLE.2).
Locate It	
How can I help students find the content in its "natural" context? Where does this skill, idea, concept, or element of content reside? What examples can they find in their own lives, with their families, and their communities? *Interconnectedness*: Acknowledgment of the eclectic and complex relationships among all things; juxtaposition • How am I connected to the concepts and ideas? How is the content I am studying related to other concepts?	Define gentrification and show images of communities (historical and current) that have experienced or are experiencing the process of gentrification. Students will work together to locate a number of local areas that are experiencing gentrification. A field trip day will be planned by students to visit the communities in search of art that is part of the gentrification process.

(continued)

Ecomindedness Lesson Plan Example *(continued)*

Teacher Thinking . . .	Students and Teacher Doing . . .
	Learn It
How can I design an experience to help students explore and experience the concept where it is found? In what ways can I help students care about themselves, others near and far, human and non-human? How can I help students understand the usefulness and meaning of this concept for their lives? *Care*: Care for self; care for animals, plants and the earth; care for family, neighbors, and strangers and distant others • What does it mean to care about myself? How does caring for myself allow me to care for others? In what ways might I care for others near and far, human and non-human?	Students will split in 2 or 3 small groups to visit gentrified communities in the metro area. Once in the local communities, students will seek out and take pictures of art that has been enacted or saved as a part of the gentrification process. Students will ask local residents and business owners questions related to positive and negative consequences associated with gentrification. In addition, students will ask about the art that has either been saved or enacted throughout the process and what that means to the community identity. Students will capture the perspectives of others, as well as those of their group, about the gentrification process and the importance of art in maintaining the historical culture and identity of the community and its members. Once returned to class, students will share pictures taken throughout the day and their learning from the day. Students will also reflect on what gentrification means to them and how, regardless of their opinion, art can be respectful and honoring of the community within the gentrification process.

Teacher Thinking . . .	Students and Teacher Doing . . .
	Live It
How can I help students think about their learning as a part of their construction of beliefs and values, along with decisionmaking? What values and beliefs are embedded in the lesson? How can I help students develop and act upon those values and beliefs? While some lessons may focus on immediate action, others may introduce a concept and generate many possibilities for living the ideas. For example, students might be introduced to thinking about habitat conservation, but the focus of the lesson is to help them connect their own habitat with animal habitats. *Integrity*: To act in accordance with one's beliefs; wholeness • How do I understand and develop my own beliefs and values related to content? What actions can I take, large and small, to act on my beliefs?	Based on student perspectives, students will create a painting on canvas that could be placed within a community experiencing gentrification. In order to truly create art that is honoring of the community, students will need to conduct some research around the history and cultural identity of their chosen area. In addition, students will need to consider the types of art that are utilized in gentrification or the points emphasized when advocating against this process. Students will share out creations as a class with explanations of the community identity captured within their piece. Students will discuss: How does art within a gentrified community respect the history and the people? How important is it to know the people in the community in order to create art that is valuing?

Notes: Consider asking parents and community members for support with this lesson.

Materials: Computers for research, transportation for field trip, canvas, paints, cameras/phones

Time and Place: 2–3 days for lesson and introduction and art creation, as well as 1 day for community visits

Place-Based Lesson Plan Example

High School Statistics , Using Statistics to Explore Local Concerns

Teacher Thinking . . .	Students and Teacher Doing . . .
Lesson Plan Element: Investigative Questions	
How might I design experiences collaboratively with students that honor their past and present experiences? Some examples: Where are we? Who lives here? How did our community form? Where does our food come from? Where do we get our drinking water? What migration patterns exist in our communities?	What are concerns in our local community? How can we explore these concerns quantitatively? Which statistical methods can we use to best represent our data to students at our school and our community?
Experience-Based Objective	
How can I describe the students' experience? Who, What, When, Where, Why, and How? Focus on the experience rather than the outcome. How will students demonstrate their understandings and developing beliefs through a multiplicity of outcomes?	Students will form organic groups based on similar interests and experiences to conduct a survey that collects quantitative data to support them in exploring a concern among members of their local community. These student-crafted quantitative survey questions may be ecological, economic, or social justice focused; for example, what percentage of land in our city is dedicated to recreation (parks, community centers, bike trails) and how does this percentage compare to other surrounding cities? What is the ratio of liquor stores to grocery stores in our city in comparison to surrounding cities? How many local businesses in our city are owned by people of color? Students will have the opportunity to research their survey question and display their data through a variety of statistical methods such as bar graphs, histograms, box and whiskers charts, landmark data (mean, mode, median), scatter plots, etc. Students will create a visual display of their research such as a poster, PowerPoint, or Prezi.

Teacher Thinking . . .	Students and Teacher Doing . . .
	Students will have the opportunity to present their findings to their classmates as well as members of the community, perhaps at a city council meeting. Students will have to consider how they will present their findings to their audience. Students will determine which statistical methods best represents the results of the data and will best connect to the audience they are presenting to. Students will write a reflection describing how choices of statistical representation can affect those consuming the data. Students will reflect and discuss how their analysis of the data through statistics influenced their perspective on the community concern they chose to research.
Direct Exploration of Places and Development of a Sense of Place	
What opportunities exist for students to explore a particular place?	Students will have the opportunity to present their work to local city leaders and members of their local community.
Multiple Pathways to Experience and Explore Ecomindedness, Including Caring, Interconnectedness, and Integrity (Optional)	
What are the pathways to experience and explore caring, interconnectedness, and integrity?	Care: Students will discuss and reflect upon how the concerns they have explored impact themselves, their school, and their community. Interconnectedness: Students will discuss how the different survey research topics chosen by their classmates are connected; e.g., how might the percentage of recreational spaces be connected to the ratio of liquor stores to grocery stores? Integrity: Students will discuss how their investigations and statistical analysis influenced the way in which they think the community concern should be approached.
Positive Action	
How can the students act to improve the situation being explored?	The class will democratically select one community concern they think they have the ability to improve or bring about wider awareness in the community. Students will develop an action plan to improve or shine light on the concern they have selected.

(continued)

Place-Based Lesson Plan Example *(continued)*

Teacher Thinking . . .	Students and Teacher Doing . . .
Inter- or Multidisciplinary Explorations	
How might I bring in interdisciplinary learning?	While this is a mathematics lesson focusing on statistical representation of data and how data representation can influence the audience viewing the data, this lesson is highly interdisciplinary depending on the research topics selected by students. Students may select community concerns that provide opportunities for them to further explore subjects such as environmental science, local history, and city politics. Due to the presentation and reflection aspects of this lesson, students will participate in interdisciplinary learning for English language arts.

Notes: Students may want to bring in articles from local journalistic sources to discuss community concerns.

Materials: Computers/iPads, Wi-Fi connection, poster, paper and pencils, coloring utensils, printer

Time and Space: This activity should take approximately 90 minutes of class time, not including the homework students complete outside of class. Extension projects such as providing students the opportunity to present their findings to the school administration and community leaders are not included in this time frame. Students can conduct research and analysis in the classroom, at the school library, and/or at home. If students select a community concern that allows for a visit to the site, planning a field trip for further investigation is an additional recommended extension activity.

Integrated Social-Emotional Learning (ISEL) Lesson Plan Template and Examples

Integrated Social-Emotional (ISEL) Lesson Plan Template

TOPIC

Teacher Thinking . . .	Students and Teacher Doing . . .
Lesson Plan Element: Integrated Social–Emotional Objective and Student SEL Objective	
What academic content am I going to cover? What SEL skill(s) will I focus on? How can I create social–emotional experiences to help students mediate the content? What kinds of personalized objectives am I hoping students will create?	
Inclusion Activity	
How can I engage the students and invite their voices into the room? What interpersonal skill can we incorporate and how might I connect that to the academic content we will cover today?	
Body of Lesson with Engaging Practices	
How am I promoting SEL? Where can we draw upon each other's experiences to make meaning? Does my lesson meet the following criteria: The activity promotes high engagement, meaning students are present and participating. Students collaborate with others for at least part of the time.	

(continued)

Integrated Social-Emotional (ISEL) Lesson Plan Template *(continued)*

Teacher Thinking . . .	Students and Teacher Doing . . .
Body of Lesson with Engaging Practices (continued)	
There are moments for creating, evaluating, reflecting, and sharing. Students are moving about for all or part of the activity rather than being sequestered in desks. Brain breaks are provided to process information, make connections, and increase transfer.	
Optimistic Closure	
How will I have students reflect on their learning in an engaging way? How will they capture their thinking and allow me to formatively assess their learning? Where can they make connections between the academic/SEL content and their lives? How will we look ahead to what's to come?	

Notes:

Time and Space:

Materials:

Integrated Social Emotional (ISEL) Lesson Plan Example

1st-Grade Social Studies: Civics and Government

Teacher Thinking . . .	Students and Teacher Doing . . .
Lesson Plan Element: Integrated Social–Emotional Objective and Student SEL Objective	
What academic content am I going to cover? What SEL skill(s) will I focus on? How can I create social–emotional experiences to help students mediate the content? What kinds of personalized objectives am I hoping students will create?	*Academic Content (Indiana Academic Standards)*: 1.2.1 Identify rights that people have and identify the responsibilities that accompany these rights. 1.2.2 Define and give examples of rules and laws in the school and the community and explain the benefits of these rules and laws. 1.2.3 Describe ways that individual actions can contribute to the common good of the classroom or community. *SEL Skill*: Self-Management By participating in a series of games, activities, and discussions, students will recognize the benefits of rules and their importance in a variety of contexts (e.g., classroom, school, community) and how self-management (regulation) can help us in this endeavor. The goal is for students to connect on a personal level regarding the use of their self-management skills to help them follow rules and better understand why it might be important to follow rules in different settings. In addition, it is important that students appreciate the rights of others, how rules help to protect those rights, and how responsible rule-following can benefit the community.

(continued)

Integrated Social Emotional (ISEL) Lesson Plan Example *(continued)*

Teacher Thinking . . .	Students and Teacher Doing . . .
Inclusion Activity	
How can I engage the students and invite their voices into the room? What interpersonal skill can we incorporate and how might I connect that to the academic content we will cover today?	Students are invited to the rug area to play several fun games. However, these games have rules that need to be followed to help make sure that everyone gets to have fun. The teacher asks for student input by prompting, "Why do you think rules are important?" and tracks student responses on chart paper. The teacher then transitions the conversation asking, "What can we all do to make sure we are following the rules and having fun? What self-management skills can we use?" (e.g., active listening, waiting your turn).
Body of Lesson with Engaging Practices	
How am I promoting SEL? Where can we draw upon each other's experiences to make meaning? Does my lesson meet the following criteria: The activity promotes high engagement, meaning students are present and participating. Students collaborate with others for at least part of the time. There are moments for creating, evaluating, reflecting, and sharing. Students are moving about for all or part of the activity rather than being sequestered in desks. Brain breaks are provided to process information, make connections, and increase transfer.	The discussion wraps up by reinforcing the self-management skills noted on the chart paper and by calling on several students to share their personal experiences using self-management skills (e.g., at the grocery store, in the car, listening to a story). The teacher leads a series of games that last only 5–10 minutes each. Before each game, the teacher discusses the rules of the game and emphasizes the self-management skill(s) related to each (e.g., standing still, being quiet, patience). The games played during this lesson include: *Simon Says, Follow the Leader, Freeze Dance, Heads Up Seven Up,* and *The Quiet Game.* At the end of each game, students circle up on the rug and briefly discuss the game and what was challenging, helpful, and fun.

Teacher Thinking . . .	Students and Teacher Doing . . .
	Midway through the series of games, the teacher prompts a brain break and leads a discussion regarding *anger* when the game doesn't "go your way." The teacher may reference an occurrence during the current games played or other frustrating situations encountered at home or school that students have shared. On a half sheet of paper, the teacher asks students to illustrate a time that they were angry and what skill they used to help alleviate that anger. After the brain break (5 minutes), the teacher continues with the remaining games for the second half.
Optimistic Closure	
How will I have students reflect on their learning in an engaging way? How will they capture their thinking and allow me to formatively assess their learning? Where can they make connections between the academic/SEL content and their lives? How will we look ahead to what's to come?	At the end of all the games, students gather on the rug. The teacher asks, "What rules do you think are important for our classroom community?" The teacher tracks responses on chart paper emphasizing positive statements versus negative (e.g., *be kind to others* versus *don't be mean*, *use an inside voice* versus *no shouting*), and help students draw a connection between positive self-management and rule following (e.g., "What do you do when . . . ? How does that help?"). With teacher guidance, students later vote on which rules they believe are *responsible* and *respectful* of everyone's *rights* and will allow all students to learn and have fun. The top 3–5 rules are selected and students sign a formal "rule poster" to be displayed in the classroom and referenced by the teacher weekly and when necessary on a group or individual basis.

Notes: Some teachers find it useful not to refer to classroom rules as "rules" and instead opt for "agreements" or "choices." The more positive the wording and involved students are in the process of their development, the higher the potential for overall student buy-in.

Materials: Games and rules, chart paper, markers, half sheets of paper, pencils, crayons, music, and poster board

Time and Space: 45–60 minutes, classroom

Integrated Social-Emotional (ISEL) Lesson Plan Example

Middle School Algebra 1, Algebraic Expressions: Combining Like Terms & Distributing

Teacher Thinking . . .	Students and Teacher Doing . . .
Lesson Plan Element: Integrated Social–Emotional Objective and Student SEL Objective	
What academic content am I going to cover? What SEL skill(s) will I focus on? How can I create social–emotional experiences to help students mediate the content? What kinds of personalized objectives am I hoping students will create?	*Academic Content*: Students will define variables, create and simplify algebraic expressions, and represent the distributive property. *SEL Skill*: Self-Management and Relationship Skills. Students will create a class recipe book out of algebraic expressions. Students will have to collaborate to ensure there is diversity in their recipe choices and algebraic expressions, as well as their use of the distributive property. Students will create personalized goals that center around time management, effective communication, and conflict resolution.
Inclusion Activity	
How can I engage the students and invite their voices into the room? What interpersonal skill can we incorporate and how might I connect that to the academic content we will cover today?	The teacher invites students to share a recipe that is personally significant to them or represents their family history or culture. The relationship skills incorporated into this lesson include active listening, teamwork, and responsibility. As a class, students discuss: • How they will participate in active listening • How they will ensure everyone in the classroom is part of the team and will have the opportunity to voice their opinions • How the class will work together to ensure the guidelines for the assignment are followed, completed with effort, and submitted by the deadline

Teacher Thinking . . .	Students and Teacher Doing . . .
Body of Lesson with Engaging Practices	
How am I promoting SEL? Where can we draw upon each other's experiences to make meaning? Does my lesson meet the following criteria: The activity promotes high engagement, meaning students are present and participating. Students collaborate with others for at least part of the time. There are moments for creating, evaluating, reflecting, and sharing. Students are moving about for all or part of the activity rather than being sequestered in desks. Brain breaks are provided to process information, make connections, and increase transfer.	Students collaborate to create a table of contents for their algebra recipe book that includes a diverse selection of foods. Students determine who is responsible for the creation of each recipe. Students work together to determine how they can represent the distributive property in a variety of ways to demonstrate mastery of the concept. Before students begin to work on their recipes individually, they must review their three interpersonal skills—active listening, teamwork, and responsibility—through group discussion. During independent work, students will be able to take advantage of the flexible seating options in the classroom. Independently, students define variables and create a recipe using algebraic expressions and the distributive property. For example, if a student selects a summer fruit salad, they might include strawberries, watermelon, lemon, blackberries, and mint. They select variables to represent each ingredient such as w = watermelon and b = blackberries. They utilize coefficients in front of their variables to communicate the quantity of each ingredient that goes into the salad such as 0.5w + 15b + 20s + 1l. Students use the distributive property to demonstrate how to reduce or increase the number of servings such as 2(0.5w + 15b + 20s + 1l) to double the recipe. After the completion of their individual recipe, students receive a brain break. After the brain break, students work with a partner to peer edit their recipe. The final draft of the recipe must be free from grammatical and mathematical errors. When all the recipes have been completed, students create a cover for their recipe book as well as a name. Students may research online for ideas and inspiration.

(continued)

Integrated Social Emotional (ISEL) Lesson Plan Example *(continued)*

Teacher Thinking . . .	Students and Teacher Doing . . .
Optimistic Closure	
How will I have students reflect on their learning in an engaging way? How will they capture their thinking and allow me to formatively assess their learning? Where can they make connections between the academic/SEL content and their lives? How will we look ahead to what's to come?	Students reflect in their learning journal through artistic or written expression. In their reflection, students address their relationship to the algebraic content of the lesson as well as the three interpersonal skills that were needed to successfully collaborate as a class. Students share their journal entries in small groups. Students lead a group discussion to determine how they would like to share their algebraic recipe book (e.g., should it be scanned and emailed to staff and students? Should select recipes be printed in the school newspaper? How might the recipe book be shared with the local community?)

Notes: Bring in sample recipes for those who may not have one of their own. Students could make their recipe as an option, but be mindful of allergies.

Materials: Computers, Wi-Fi connection, printer or pencil and paper, and coloring utensils

Time and Space: This activity should take about 60 minutes. Extra time could be provided to allow for more work on the appearance of the recipes and book cover. Extension activities such as sharing the recipe book with the school and/or local community are not included in this time frame. This activity can occur in the classroom, the school library, and at students' homes as a complement to other larger school initiatives.

Integrated Social-Emotional (ISEL) Lesson Plan Example

High School Science, Reflection and Responsible Decisionmaking

Teacher Thinking . . .	Students and Teacher Doing . . .
	Lesson Plan Element: ***Integrated Social–Emotional Objective and Student SEL Objective***
What academic content am I going to cover? What SEL skill(s) will I focus on? How can I create social–emotional experiences to help students mediate the content? What kinds of personalized objectives am I hoping students will create?	*Academic Content (Colorado Academic Standards)*: Students will review research and case studies on regional catastrophic events and the relationship between plate movement and potential geologic hazards in order to propose proactive solutions for highly populated areas with increased plate activity. HS.3.3 The theory of plate tectonics helps to explain geological, physical, and geographical features of Earth HS.3.7 Natural hazards have local, national, and global impacts such as volcanoes, earthquakes, tsunamis, hurricanes, and thunderstorms *SEL Skill*: Responsible decisionmaking is the focus of this lesson, including identifying problems, analyzing situations, and solving problems. Students will also work on relationship skills through collaboration and teamwork.
	Inclusion Activity
How can I engage the students and invite their voices into the room? What interpersonal skill can we incorporate and how might I connect that to the academic content we will cover today?	Present videos and pictures for students about catastrophic events and natural disasters. Provide time for students to circle up in groups of 4–5 people to discuss the outcomes of the catastrophic events and to describe the impact on people. Before moving to the next activity, the teacher discusses the importance of responsible decisionmaking and the impact on society. As a part of responsible decisionmaking, the teacher describes ways to identify problems through analysis and ways to solve problems through a problem-solution chart. In addition, the teacher emphasizes the importance of collaboration and the qualities of good teamwork (including turn-taking and perspective-taking).

(continued)

Integrated Social Emotional (ISEL) Lesson Plan Example *(continued)*

Teacher Thinking . . .	Students and Teacher Doing . . .
	Body of Lesson with Engaging Practices
How am I promoting SEL? Where can we draw upon each other's experiences to make meaning? Does my lesson meet the following criteria: The activity promotes high engagement, meaning students are present and participating. Students collaborate with others for at least part of the time. There are moments for creating, evaluating, reflecting, and sharing. Students are moving about for all or part of the activity rather than being sequestered in desks. Brain breaks are provided to process information, make connections, and increase transfer.	Provide students with time to review research and case studies around 5 or 6 tectonic-related catastrophes or natural disasters. Each group is assigned one catastrophe/natural disaster (e.g., tsunami group, earthquake group). As a class, discuss the connections between natural hazards and tectonic activity. Have students form small groups around the catastrophe or natural disaster they studied. Students explore the cause and effect relationship between tectonic activity and their identified event while capturing answers on a T-Chart. Students discuss 4–5 outcomes that had an immediate effect on people. Each outcome will be captured as a problem on a separate problem-solution chart. As a group, students come up with proactive strategies that could have alleviated or mediated the disastrous outcome. Once all groups have completed their problem-solution chart, students form new groups with one representative from each of the catastrophe/natural disaster groups. For example, the new group might have one representative from the tsunamis group and one representative from the earthquake group, as opposed to two representatives from the same group. In order to find a new group, students number off. A timer is set and students have 60 seconds to quickly form a new group with every number represented only once. Within this new group, students share their problem-solving solutions.

<table>
<tr><th>Teacher Thinking . . .</th><th>Students and Teacher Doing . . .</th></tr>
<tr><td colspan="2">Optimistic Closure</td></tr>
<tr><td>How will I have students reflect on their learning in an engaging way? How will they capture their thinking and allow me to formatively assess their learning? Where can they make connections between the academic/SEL content and their lives? How will we look ahead to what's to come?</td><td>After groups have had the opportunity for each representative to share out, the class comes back together to identify similarities and differences between their solutions.

The students then have a discussion around the importance of analyzing past problems to create solutions for the future. Students will consider the following questions:
• How important is it to analyze available data in order to determine possible solutions?
• What is the importance of reviewing catastrophes and natural disasters of the past?
Considering the importance of analyzing details and reflecting on the past lays the foundation for a discussion around how students can learn from their own experiences. Close with an opportunity for students to discuss how responsible decisionmaking can help them in their own lives. Ask them to talk to other adults in their lives about decisionmaking and bring back what they learned for a future class discussion.</td></tr>
</table>

Notes: Before the lesson, it might be helpful to review qualities of good teamwork.

Materials: Videos and pictures for students about catastrophic events and natural disasters, problem-solution chart, T-chart, 5–6 research and case studies on tectonic-related catastrophes or natural disasters

Time and Space: 1 or 2 class periods, depending on work production of students, space to work in groups

References

Almerico, G., Johnston, P., Henriott, D., & Shapiro, M. (2011). Dispositions assessment in teacher education: Developing an assessment instrument for the college classroom and the field. *Research in Higher Education Journal, 11*. Retrieved from www.aabri.com/manuscripts/10665.pdf

Ames, C. (1992). Classrooms: Goals, structures and student motivation. *Journal of Educational Psychology, 84,* 261–271.

Anderman, L. H., & Freeman, T. M. (2004). Students' sense of belonging in school. In M. Maehr & P. R. Pintrich (Eds.), *Advances in Motivation and Achievement: Volume 13. Motivating Students, Improving Schools: The Legacy of Carol Midgley* (pp. 27–63). Oxford, England: Elsevier, JAI.

Anderson, J. R., Greeno, J. G., Reder, L. M., & Simon, H. A. (2000). Perspectives on learning, thinking, and activity. *Educational Researcher, 29*(4), 11–13.

Anderson, J. R., Reder, L. M., & Simon, H. A. (1998). Radical constructivism and cognitive psychology. *Brookings Papers on Education Policy, 1*(1998), 227–278.

Arnheim, R. (1989). *Thoughts on art education* [Mimeo]. Los Angeles, CA: J. Paul Getty Center for Education in the Arts.

Bain, H. P., & Jacobs, R. (1990). *The case for smaller classes and better teachers* (DHHS Publication No. ISSN-0735-0023). Washington, DC: National Association of Secondary School Principals Printing Office.

Banks, J. A. (2002). *An introduction to multicultural education.* Boston, MA: Allyn and Bacon.

Banks, J. A. (2004). Teaching for social justice, diversity, and citizenship in a global world. *The Education Forum, 68*(1), 289–298.

Barber, B. K., & Olsen, J. A. (2004). Assessing the transition to middle and high school. *Journal of Adolescent Research, 19,* 3–30.

Bartolomé, L. (1994). Beyond the methods fetish: Toward a humanizing pedagogy. *Harvard Educational Review, 64,* 173–194.

Baxter, K. (2019). *Creating vibrant art lesson plans: A teacher's sketchbook.* New York, NY: Teachers College Press.

Bennett, C. (2001). Genres of research in multicultural education. *Review of Educational Research, 71*(2), 171–217.

Blumenfeld, P. C. (1992). Classroom learning and motivation: Clarifying and expanding goal theory. *Journal of Educational Psychology, 84,* 272–281.

Boggess, L. (2010). Tailoring new urban teachers for character and activism. *American Educational Research Journal, 47*(1), 65–95.

Bondy, E., Ross, D., Gallingane, C, & Hambacher, E. (2007). Creating environments of success and resilience: Culturally responsive classroom management and more. *Urban Education, 42*(4), 326–348.

Borden, R. (2014). Increasing mentoring skills of cooperating teachers to enhance support for pre-service teacher candidates (Doctoral dissertation). Retrieved from Arizona State University Repository. (134811)

Boshkoff, R. (1991). Lesson planning the Kodaly way. *Music Educators Journal, 78*(2), 20–34.

Brooks, J. G., & Brooks, M. G. (1999). *In search of understanding: The case for constructivist classrooms* (2nd ed.). Alexandria, VA: ASCD.

Brophy, J. (1983). Conceptualizing student motivation. *Educational Psychology, 18*, 200–215.

Brophy, J., & Good, T. (1974). *Teacher-student relationships: Causes and consequences.* New York, NY: Holt, Rinehart & Winston.

Brown, M. R. (2007). Educating all students: Creating culturally responsive teachers, classrooms, and schools. *Intervention in School and Clinic, 43*(1), 57–62.

Bruner, J. (1960). *The process of education.* Cambridge, MA: Harvard University Press.

Castagno, A. E., & McKinley, B. (2008). Culturally responsive schooling for indigenous youth: A review of the literature. *Review of Educational Research, 78*(4), 941–993.

Center for Applied Special Technology. (1998). What is universal design for learning? Retrieved from www.udlcenter.org/aboutudl

Centers for Disease Control and Prevention. (2019). *Data and statistics on children's mental health.* Retrieved from www.cdc.gov/childrensmentalhealth/data.html

Child & Adolescent Health Measurement Initiative. (2017). *Adverse childhood experiences among U.S. children.* Retrieved from www.cahmi.org/wp-content/uploads/2018/05/aces_fact_sheet.pdf

Collaborative for Academic, Social, and Emotional Learning. (2017). *Sample teaching activities to support core competencies of social and emotional learning.* Retrieved from www.casel.org/wp-content/uploads/2017/08/Sample-Teaching-Activities-to-Support-Core-Competencies-8-20-17.pdf

Collaborative for Academic, Social, and Emotional Learning. (2019). *An examination of frameworks for social and emotional learning (SEL) reflected in state K–12 learning standards.* Retrieved from measuringsel.casel.org/wp-content/uploads/2019/02/Framework-C.3.pdf

Collaborative for Academic, Social, and Emotional Learning. (n.d.). *Core SEL competencies.* Retrieved from casel.org/core-competencies/

Collaborative for Academic, Social, and Emotional Learning. (n.d.) *History.* Retrieved from: casel.org/history/

Collier, M. D. (2005). An ethic of caring: the fuel for high teacher efficacy. *The Urban Review, 37*(4), 351–359.

Combs, A. W. (1974). Humanistic goals of education. In I. D. Welch, F. Richards, & A. C. Richards (Eds.), *Educational accountability: A humanistic perspective.* San Francisco, CA: Shields.

Comer, J. P. (1980). *School power: Implications of an intervention project.* New York, NY: The Free Press.

Connelly, F. M., & Clandinin, D.J. (1988). *Teachers as curriculum planners: Narratives of experience.* New York, NY: Teachers College Press.

Conrad, B. (2011). *Intentions, operations, beliefs, & dispositions of teachers at culturally diverse schools: Examining the intricacies and complexities of great teachers* (Publication no. 140, doctoral dissertation). University of Denver, Electronic Theses and Dissertations.

Conrad, B. (2012). Intentions and beliefs: Why they matter and a conceptual framework for understanding them in culturally responsive teachers. *Curriculum and Teaching Dialogue, 14*(1), 85–97.

Conrad, B. (in press). Constructivism. In *Encyclopedia of curriculum.* New York, NY: Routledge. (Expected Fall 2020)

Conrad, B., & Shalter-Bruening, P. (2016, April 10). *Improving teacher evaluations and training: A blueprint for comprehensive assessment of teacher dispositions.* Paper presented at the 2016 Annual Meeting of the American Educational Research Association, Washington, DC.

Conrad, B., & Shalter-Bruening, P. (2019). A reconceptualization of effective teacher dispositions from a culturally responsive and an educational psychology perspective. (*Submitted for review, 2019.*)

Conrad, B., Uhrmacher, P. B., & Moroye, C. M. (2015). Curriculum disruption: A vision for new practices in teaching and learning. *Journal of Scholastic Inquiry: Education, 18*(3), 1–20.

Craig, S. E. (2008). *Reaching and teaching children who hurt: Strategies for your classroom.* Baltimore, MD: Paul H. Brookes.

Csikszentmihalyi, M., & Robinson, R. E. (1990). *The art of seeing: An interpretation of the aesthetic encounter.* Los Angeles, CA: Getty Publications.

Culture. (2019). In *Lexico.com*. Retrieved from www.lexico.com/en/definition/culture

Curtis, J. (2017). We know SEL skills are important, so how the heck do we measure them? Retrieved from www.edsurge.com/news/2017-05-09-we-know-sel-skills-are-important-so-how-the-heck-do-we-measure-them

Darling-Hammond, L. (2015). Social and emotional learning: Critical skills for building healthy schools. In J. A. Durlak, C. E. Domitrovich, R. P. Weissberg, & T. P. Gullotta (Eds.), *Handbook of social and emotional learning: Research and practice* (xi–xiv). New York: Guilford Press.

Darling-Hammond, L., & Cook-Harvey, C. M. (2018). *Educating the whole child: Improving school climate to support student success.* Palo Alto, CA: Learning Policy Institute.

Davis, H. A. (2003). Conceptualizing the role and influence of student-teacher relationships on children's social and cognitive development. *Educational Psychologist, 38,* 207–234.

De Bono. E. (1970). *Lateral thinking: A textbook of creativity.* London, U.K.: Ward Lock Educational.

Deci, E. L., Vallerand, R. J., Pelletier, L.G., & Ryan, R. M. (1991). Motivation and Education: The self-determination perspective. *Educational Psychologist, 26,* 325–346.

Delpit, L. (2006). *Other people's children: Cultural conflict in the classroom.* New York, NY: The New Press.

Demarest, A. B. (2015). *Place-based curriculum design: Exceeding standards through local investigations.* New York, NY: Routledge.

DePorter, B., & Hernacki, M. (1992). *Quantum learning: Unleashing the genius in you.* New York, NY: Random House.

DePorter, B., Reardon, M., & Singer-Nourie, S. (1999). *Quantum teaching.* Needham Heights, MA: Allyn & Bacon.

Dewey, J. (1938). *Art as experience.* New York, NY: Perigee Books.

Duckworth, E. (2009). Helping students get to where ideas can find them. *The New Educator, 5*(3), 185–188.

Durlak, J. A., Weissberg, R. P., Dymnicki, A, B. Taylor, R. D., & Schellinger, K. B. (2011). The impact of enhancing students' social and emotional learning: A meta-analysis of school-based universal interventions. *Child Development, 82*(1), 405–432.

Dusenbury, L., Calin, S., Domitrovich, C., & Weissberg, R. P. (2015). What does evidence-based instruction in social and emotional learning actually look like in practice? *A Brief on Findings from CASEL's Program Reviews,* 1–6.

Dweck, C. S. (2006). *Mindset: The new psychology of success.* New York, NY: Random House.

Ecological. (2019). In *Oxford English Dictionary Online.* Retrieved from www-oed-com.unco.idm.oclc.org/view/Entry/249591?redirectedFrom=ecological#eid

Eisner, E. W. (1967). Instructional and expressive educational objectives: Their formulation and use in curriculum. (ED028838).

Eisner, E. W. (1994). *Curriculum and cognition reconsidered.* New York, NY: Teachers College Press.

Eisner, E. W. (2002). *The educational imagination: On the design and evaluation of school programs* (4th ed.). New York, NY: Macmillan.

Eisner, E. W. (2005). *Reimagining schools: The selected works of Elliot W. Eisner.* New York, NY: Routledge.

Elias, M. J., Zins, J. E., & Weissberg, R. P. (1997). *Promoting social and emotional learning: Guidelines for educators.* Alexandria, VA: ASCD.

Ellis, A. K., & Bond, J. B. (2016). *Research on educational innovations* (5th ed.). New York, NY: Routledge.

Erickson, F. (1987). Transformation and school success: The politics and culture of educational achievement. *Anthropology and Education Quarterly, 18,* 335–356.

Fairbanks, C. M., Duffy, G. G., He, Y., Levin, B., Rohr, J., & Stein, C. (2010). Beyond knowledge: Exploring why some teachers are more thoughtfully adaptive than others. *Journal of Teacher Education. 61*(1–2), 161–171.

Fisher, D., & Frey, N. (2013). *Better learning through structured teaching: A framework for the gradual release of responsibility* (2nd ed.). Alexandria, VA: ASCD.

Flinders, D. J., & Thornton, S. J. (2012). *The curriculum studies reader* (4th ed.) New York, NY: Routledge.

Fraser, B. J., & Fisher, D. L. (1982). Predicting students' outcomes from their perceptions of classroom psychosocial environment. *American Educational Research Journal, 19,* 498–518.

Freire, P. (1970). *Pedagogy of the oppressed.* New York, NY: Continuum.

Gabler, I. C., & Schroeder, M. (Eds.). (2003). *Constructivist methods for the secondary classroom.* Boston, MA: Pearson.

Galluzzo, G. R. (1999, May 5). Will the best and brightest teach? *Education Week.* Retrieved from www.edweek.org/ew/articles/1999/05/05/34galluz.h18.html

Gardner, H. (1983). *Frames of mind: The theory of multiple intelligences.* New York, NY: Basic Books.

Garmon, M. A. (2004). Changing preservice teachers' attitudes/beliefs about diversity: What are the critical factors? *Journal of Teacher Education, 55*(3), 201–213.

Gay, G. (1997). Multicultural infusion in teacher education: Foundations and applications. *Peabody Journal of Education.* 72(1), 150–177.

Gay, G. (2000). *Culturally responsive teaching: Theory, research, & practice.* New York, NY: Teachers College Press.

Germain, M. H. (1998). *Worldly teachers: Cultural learning and pedagogy.* Westport, CT: Bergin & Garvey.

Goleman, D. (1995). *Emotional intelligence: Why it can matter more than IQ.* New York, NY: Bantam.

Graff, N. (2011). "An effective and agonizing way to learn": Backwards design and new teachers' preparation for planning curriculum. *Teacher Education Quarterly, 38*(3), 151–168.

Greene, M. (2001). *Variations on a blue guitar: The Lincoln Center Institute lectures on aesthetic education.* New York, NY: Teachers College Press.

Grennon Brooks, J. (2004) Constructivism as a paradigm for teaching and learning. Retrieved from www.thirteen.org/edonline/concept2class/constructivism/index.html

Gross, R., & Gross, B. (1969). *Radical school reform.* New York, NY: Simon and Schuster.

Haberman, M., Gillette, M. D., & Hill, D. A. (2017). *Star teachers of children in poverty* (2nd ed.). New York, NY: Routledge.

He, M. F., Phillion, J., Chan, E., & Xu, S. (2008). Immigrant students' experience of curriculum. In F. M. Connelly, M. F. He, & J. Phillion (Eds.), *The SAGE handbook of curriculum and instruction.* (pp. 219–239). Los Angeles, CA: Sage.

Hernandez Sheets, R. (1995). From remedial to gifted: Effects of culturally centered pedagogy. *Theory into Practice, 34*(3), 186–193.

Hirsch, E. D., Jr. (1996). *The schools we need and why we don't have them.* New York, NY: Doubleday.

Hlebowitsh, P. (2001). *Foundations of American education: Purpose and promise* (2nd ed.). Belmont, CA: Wadsworth.

Hlebowitsh, P. (2013). Foreword. In R. W. Tyler, *Basic principles of curriculum and instruction* (Revised ed., pp. vii–xii). Chicago, IL: University of Chicago Press.

hooks, b. (1994). *Teaching to transgress: Education as the practice of freedom.* New York, NY: Routledge.

Howard, G. (2018). *We can't teach what we don't know: White teachers, multiracial schools* (3rd ed). New York, NY: Teachers College Press.

Hunter, M. (1967). *Teach more—faster!* El Segundo, CA: TIP Publications.

Hunter, M. (1983) *Mastery teaching*. El Segundo, CA: TIP Publications.

Ingman, B. C., & McConnell Moroye, C. (2019). Experience-based objectives. *Educational Studies 55*(3), 346–367.

Jarvis, P. (2006). *The theory and practice of teaching*. New York, NY: Routledge.

Jennings, P. A. (2018). *The trauma-sensitive classroom: Building resilience with compassionate teaching*. New York, NY: Norton & Co.

Jones, S., Brush, K., Bailey, R., Brion-Meisels, G., McIntyre, J., Kahn, J., Nelson, B., & Stickle, L. (2017). *Navigating SEL from the inside out: Looking inside and across 25 leading SEL programs: A practical resource for schools and OST providers*. Cambridge, MA: Harvard Graduate School of Education. Retrieved from www.wallacefoundation.org/knowledge-center/documents/navigating-social-and-emotional-learning-from-the-inside-out.pdf

Juvonen, J. (2006). Sense of belonging, social bonds, and school functioning. In P. A. Alexander & P. H. Winne (Eds.). *Handbook of educational psychology* (pp. 655–674). Mahwah, NJ: Lawrence Erlbaum Associates.

Kaplan, A., Middleton, M. J., Urdan, T., & Midgley, C. (2002). Achievement goals and goal structures. In C. Midgley (Ed.), *Goals, goal structures, and patterns of adaptive learning* (pp. 21–53). Mahwah, NJ: Lawrence Erlbaum Associates.

Kluckhohn, C. K. M., & Murray, H. A. (1953). Personality formation: The determinants. In C. K. M. Kluckhohn & H. A. Murray (Eds.), *Personality in nature, society and culture* (pp. 53–70). New York, NY: Alfred A. Knopf.

Ladson-Billings, G. (1992). Reading between the lines and beyond the pages: A culturally relevant approach to literacy teaching. *Theory into Practice, 31*(4), 312–319.

Ladson-Billings, G. (1994). *The dreamkeepers: Successful teachers of African American children*. San Francisco, CA: Jossey-Bass.

Ladson-Billings, G. (1995). But that's just good teaching! The case for culturally relevant pedagogy. *Theory into Practice, 34*(3), 159–165.

Lane-Zucker, L. (2004). Foreword. In D. Sobel, *Place based education: Connecting classrooms and communities* (pp. i–iv). Great Barrington, MA: Orion Society.

Lewis, C. W., James, M., Hancock, S., & Hill-Jackson, V. (2008). Framing African American students' success and failure in urban settings: A typology for change. *Urban Education. 43*(2), 127–153.

Lipman, P. (1995). "Bringing out the best in them": The contribution of culturally relevant teachers to educational reform. *Theory into Practice, 34*(3), 202–208.

Madeja, S. S., & Onuska, S. (1977). *Through the arts to the aesthetic: The CEMREL aesthetic education curriculum*. St. Louis, MO: CEMREL.

Martusewicz, R. (2005). Special issue: EcoJustice and education. *Educational Studies 38*(1), 1–5.

Marzano, R. J., Pickering, D. J., & McTighe, J. (1993). *Assessing student outcomes: Performance assessment using the dimensions of learning model*. Alexandria, VA: ASCD.

Marzano, R. J., Pickering, D. J., & Pollock, J. E. (2001). *Classroom instruction that works: Research-based strategies for increasing student achievement*. Alexandria, VA: ASCD.

Mayer, J. D., Salovey, P., Caruso, D. R., & Cherkasskiy, L. (2011). Emotional intelligence. In R. J. Sternberg & S. B. Kaufman (Eds.), *The Cambridge handbook of intelligence* (pp. 528–549). New York, NY: Cambridge University Press.

McAllister, G., & Irvine, J. J. (2002). The role of empathy in teaching culturally diverse students: A qualitative study of teachers' beliefs. *Journal of Teacher Education. 53*(5), 433–443.

McConnell Moroye, C., & Ingman, B. C. (2018). Ecologically minded teaching. *Environmental Education Research, 24*(8), 1128–1142.

McLeod, S. A. (2019). Bruner—Learning theory in education. Retrieved from www.simplypsychology.org/bruner.html

Michalec, P. (2013). Common Core and inner core. *Curriculum & Teaching Dialogue, 15*(1/2).

Middleton, M. J., & Midgley, C. (2002). Beyond motivation: Middle school students' perceptions of press for understanding in math. *Contemporary Educational Psychology, 27,* 373–391.

Minnesota Department of Education. (2018). Social and emotional learning assessment guidance. Retrieved from education.mn.gov/MDE/dse/safe/social/imp/

Moore, K. D. (2009). *Effective instructional strategies: From theory to practice.* Los Angeles, CA: Sage.

Moos, R. H., & Moos, B. S. (1978). Classroom social climate and student absences and grades. *Journal of Educational Psychology, 70,* 263–269.

Moroye, C. M. (2009). Complementary curriculum: the work of ecologically minded teachers. *Journal of Curriculum Studies, 41*(6), 789-811.

Moroye, C. M. (2010). Ecologically-minded teaching: Authenticity and care. In P. B. Uhrmacher & K. Bunn (Eds.), *Beyond the one room school* (pp. 97–114). Rotterdam, NL: Sense.

Moroye, C. M., & Ingman, B. C. (2013). Ecological mindedness across the curriculum. *Curriculum Inquiry, 43*(5), 588–612.

Moroye, C. M., & Uhrmacher, P. B. (2009). Aesthetic themes of education. *Curriculum and Teaching Dialogue, 11*(1–2), 85–101.

Moroye, C. M., & Uhrmacher, P. B. (2010). Aesthetic themes as conduits to creativity. In C. Craig & L. F. Dertechin (Eds.), *Cultivating curious and creative minds, The role of teachers and teacher educators: Part 1* (pp. 99–114). Teacher Education Yearbook XVIII. Lanham, MD: Rowman & Littlefield Education,

National Child Traumatic Stress Network (2008). *Child trauma toolkit for educators.* Retrieved from wmich.edu/sites/default/files/attachments/u57/2013/child-trauma-toolkit.pdf

National Commission on Excellence in Education. (1983). *A nation at risk: The imperative for educational reform: A report to the nation and the Secretary of Education, United States Department of Education.* Washington, DC: The Commission. [Supt. of Docs., U.S. G.P.O. distributor].

Nickerson, A. B. (2018). Can SEL reduce school violence? *Educational Leadership, 76*(2), 46–50.

Nickerson, A. B., Fredrick, S., Allen, K. & Jenkins, L. (2019). Social emotional learning (SEL) practices in schools: Effects on perceptions of bullying victimization. *Journal of School Psychology, 73,* 74–88.

Nieto, S. (Ed.). (2005). *Why we teach.* New York, NY: Teachers College Press.

Nieto, S. (1999). *A light in their eyes: Creating multicultural learning communities.* New York, NY: Teachers College Press.

Nieto, S., & Bode, P. (2018). *Affirming diversity: The sociopolitical context of multicultural education.* Boston, MA: Pearson.

Noddings, N. (1992). *The challenge to care in schools: An alternative approach to education.* New York, NY: Teachers College Press.

Osborne, A. B. (1996). Practice into theory into practice: Culturally relevant pedagogy for students we have marginalized and normalized. *Anthropology & Education Quarterly, 27*(3), 285–314.

Palmer, J. (1998). *Environmental education in the 21st century: Theory, practice, progress and promise.* London, England: Routledge.

Palmer, P. (2017). *The courage to teach: Exploring the inner landscape of a teacher's life* (20th anniversary edition). San Francisco, CA: Jossey-Bass.

Park, D. (1995). *Combining satellite education and a STISE pedagogical model to enhance elementary science teaching in Korea and the United States* (Unpublished master's thesis). West Chester University of Pennsylvania.

Patrick, H., Anderman, L. H., & Ryan, A. M. (2002). Social motivation and the classroom social environment. In C. Midgley (Ed.), *Goals, goal structures, and patterns of adaptive learning* (pp. 85–104). Mahwah, NJ: Lawrence Erlbaum Associates.

Pearson, P. D., & Gallagher, G. (1983). The gradual release of responsibility model of instruction. *Contemporary Educational Psychology, 8*, 112–123.

Perry, N. E., Turner, J. C., & Meyer, D. K. (2006). Classrooms as contexts for motivating learning. In P. A. Alexander & P. H. Winne (Eds.), *Handbook of educational psychology* (2nd ed., pp. 327–348). Mahwah, NJ: Lawrence Erlbaum.

Phillips, D. C., Ed. (2000). *Constructivism in education: Opinions and second opinions on controversial issues.* Chicago, IL: National Society for the Study of Education.

Raver, C. C., & Knitzer, J. (2002). *Ready to enter: What research tells policy makers about strategies to promote social and emotional school readiness among three and four-year-olds.* Washington, DC: National Center for Children in Poverty.

Read, H. (1966). *The redemption of the robot: My encounter with education through art.* London, England: Faber and Faber.

Reeve, J. (2006). Teachers as facilitators: What autonomy-supportive teachers do and why their students benefit. *The Elementary School Journal, 106*, 225–236.

Rosenshine, B. (2008). *Five meanings of direct instruction.* Lincoln, IL: Center on Innovation & Instruction. Retrieved from www.researchgate.net/publication/254957371_Five_Meanings_of_Direct_Instruction

Sachs, S. K. (2004). Evaluation of teacher attitudes as predictors of success in urban schools. *Journal of Teacher Education, 55*(2), 177–187.

Sadker, D., & Zittleman, K. (2016). *Teachers, schools and society: A brief introduction to Education* (4th ed.). New York, NY: McGraw-Hill.

Salovey, P., & Mayer, J. D. (1990). Emotional intelligence. *Imagination, Cognition, and Personality, 9*(3), 185–211.

Schunk, D. H. (2016). *Learning theories: An educational perspective* (8th ed.). Hoboken, NJ: Pearson.

Schunk, D. H., & Pajares, F. (2004). Self-efficacy in education revisited: Empirical and applied evidence. In D. M. McInerney & S. Van Etten (Eds.), *Big theories revisited* (pp. 115–138). Greenwich, CT: Information Age.

Shalter-Bruening, P., & Conrad, B. (2014, October). Reconceptualization of effective teacher dispositions from a culturally responsive and an educational psychology perspective. Paper presented at American Association for Teaching and Curriculum Annual Conference, Tampa, FL.

Shiveley, J., & Misco, T. (2010). But how do I know about their attitudes and beliefs?: A four-step process for integrating and assessing dispositions in teacher education. *The Clearing House, 83*(1), 9–14.

Shulman, L. S. (1986). Those who understand: Knowledge growth in teaching. *Educational Researcher, 15*(2), 4–14

Sklad, M., Diekstra, R., De Ritter, M., Ben, J., & Gravesteijn, C. (2012). Effectiveness of school-based universal social, emotional, and behavioral programs. Do they enhance students' development in the area of skill, behavior, and adjustment? *Psychology and Schools, 49*, 892–909.

Sleeter, C. (2008). An invitation to support diverse students through teacher education. *Journal of Teacher Education. 59*(3), 212–219.

Smith, G. A. (2007). Place based education: Breaking through the constraining regularities of public school. *Environmental Education Research, 13*(2), 189–207.

Sobel, D. (1996). *Beyond ecophobia: Reclaiming the heart in nature education.* Great Barrington, MA: The Orion Society.

Sockett, H. (2006). Character, rules, and regulations. In H. Sockett (Ed.), *Building a teacher education framework of moral standards* (pp. 9–26). Washington, DC: The American Association of Colleges for Teacher Education.

Solomon, D., Battistich, V., Kim, D. & Watson, M. (1997). Teacher practices associated with students' sense of the classroom as a community. *Social Psychology of Education, 1*, 235–267.

Srinivasan, M. (2018). *SEL every day: Integrating social and emotional learning with instruction in secondary classrooms.* New York, NY: Norton & Co.

Sterling, S. (2001). *Sustainable education: Re-visioning learning and change.* Bristol, UK: Schumacher.

Storz, M. G., & Nestor, K. R. (2008). It's all about relationships: Urban middle school students speak out on effective schooling practices. In F. P. Peterman (Ed.), *Preparing to prepare urban teachers* (77–101). New York, NY: Peter Lang.

Stotko, E. M., Ingram, R., & Beaty-O'Ferrall, M. E. (2007). Promising strategies for attracting and retaining successful urban teachers. *Urban Education, 42*(1), 30–51.

Swartz, E. (2005). Teaching White preservice teachers: Pedagogy for change. *Urban Education, 38*(3), 255–278.

Talbert-Johnson, C. (2004). Structural inequities and the achievement gap in urban schools. *Education and Urban Society, 37*(1), 22–36.

Talbert-Johnson, C. (2006). Preparing highly qualified teacher candidates for urban schools: The importance of dispositions. *Education and Urban Society, 39*(1), 147–160.

Taliaferro Baszile, D. (2017). In pursuit of the revolutionary-not-yet: Some thoughts on education work, movement, building, and praxis. *Educational Studies, 53*(3), 206–215. doi:10.1080/00131946.2017.1307197

Taylor, J. J., Buckley, K., Hamilton, L. S., Stecher, B. M., Read, L., & Schweig, J. (2018). *Choosing and using SEL competency assessments: What schools and districts need to know.* Retrieved from measuringsel.casel.org/pdf/Choosing-and-Using-SEL-Competency-Assessments_What-Schools-and-Districts-Need-to-Know.pdf

Taylor, R. D., Oberle, E., Durlak, J. A., & Weissberg, R. P. (2017). Promoting positive youth development through school-based social and emotional learning interventions: A meta-analysis of follow-up effects. *Child Development, 88*(4), 1156–1171.

Taylor, R. L., & Wasicsko, M. M. (2000, November). *The dispositions to teach.* Paper presented at the annual meeting of the Southern Region Association of Teacher Educators Conference, Lexington, KY.

Thompson, S., Ransdell, M., & Rousseau, C. (2005). Effective teachers in urban school settings: Linking teacher disposition and student performance on standardized tests. *Journal of Authentic Learning, 2*(1), 22–34.

Thorndike, E. L. (1920). Intelligence and its uses. *Harper's Magazine, 140,* 227–235.

Tilbury, D. (1995). Environmental education for sustainability: Defining the new focus of environmental education in the 1990s. *Environmental Education Research, 1*(2), 195–212.

Tomlinson, C. A. (1999). *The differentiated classroom: Responding to the needs of all learners.* Alexandria, VA: Association for Supervision and Curriculum Development.

Tricarico, K., & Yendol-Hoppey, D. (2011). Teacher learning through self-regulation: An exploratory study of alternative prepared teachers' ability to plan differentiated instruction in an urban elementary school. *Teacher Education Quarterly 39*(1), 139–158.

Ttofi, M. M., Bowes, L., Farrington, D. P., & Lösel, F. (2014). Protective factors interrupting the continuity from school bullying to later internalizing and externalizing problems: A systematic review of prospective longitudinal studies. *Journal of School Violence, 13,* 5–38.

Turner, J. C., & Meyer, D. K. (2004). Are challenge and caring compatible in middle school mathematics classrooms? In M. Maehr & P. Pintrich (Eds.), *Advances in motivation and achievement: Volume 13. Motivating students, improving schools: The legacy of Carol Midgley* (pp. 331–360). Oxford, U.K.: Elsevier, JAI.

Turner, J. C., & Patrick, H. (2004). Motivational influences on student participation in classroom learning activities. *Teachers College Record, 106,* 1759–1785.

Tyler, R. (1949). *Basic principles of curriculum and instruction.* Chicago, IL: University of Chicago Press.

Uhrmacher, P. B. (2009). Toward a theory of aesthetic learning experiences. *Curriculum Inquiry, 39*(5), 613–636.

Uhrmacher, P. B., & Bunn, K. (Eds.). (2011). *Beyond the one room school.* Rotterdam, NL: Sense Publications.

Uhrmacher, P. B., Conrad, B., & Moroye, C. M. (2013). Finding the balance between process and product in lesson planning: The perceptual lesson planning model. *Teachers College Record, 115*(7), 1–27.

Uhrmacher, P. B., & Moroye, C. M. (2007). Instituting the arts. *The Clearing House, 81*(2), 53–58.

Uhrmacher, P. B., McConnell Moroye, C., & Flinders, D. J. (2017). *Using educational criticism and connoisseurship for qualitative research.* New York, NY: Routledge.

VanAusdal, K. (2019). Collaborative classrooms support social–emotional learning. *ASCD Express, 14*(22). Retrieved from www.ascd.org/ascd-express/vol14/num22/collaborative-classrooms-support-social-emotional-learning.aspx

Villegas, A. M., & Lucas, T. (2002). *Educating culturally responsive teachers: A coherent approach.* Albany, NY: State University of New York Press.

Vygotsky, L. S. (1978). *Mind in society.* Cambridge, MA: Harvard University Press.

Walker, J. M. T. (2008). Looking at teacher practices through the lens of parenting style. *The Journal of Experimental Education*, 76(2), 218–240.

Ward-Roncalli, S. (2018). *How social emotional learning can mitigate the effects of trauma* [Blog post]. *TransformEd.* Retrieved from www.transformingeducation.org/how-social-emotional-learning-can-mitigate-the-effects-of-trauma/

Wasicsko, M. M. (2002). *Assessing educator dispositions: A perceptual psychological approach.* Retrieved from inside.nku.edu/content/dam/coehs/old/docs/dispositions/resources/Manual103.pdf

Waxman, H., Padrón, Y., & Arnold, K. (2001). Effective instructional practices for students placed at risk of academic failure. In G. Borman, S. Stringfield, & R. Slavin (Eds.), *Title I: Compensatory education at the crossroads* (pp. 201–223). New York, NY: Academic Press.

We Are Teachers (2020). Ten things about childhood trauma every teacher needs to know. Retrieved from www.weareteachers.com/10-things-about-childhood-trauma-every-teacher-needs-to-know/

Weegar, M. A., & Pacis, D. (2012). *A comparison of two theories of learning: Behaviorism and constructivism as applied to face-to-face and online learning* [Ebook]. San Diego, CA: E-Leader, Manila. Retrieved from www.g-casa.com/conferences/manila/papers/Weegar.pdf

Weiner, L. (1997). New teachers: Designing lesson plans: What new teachers can learn from Moffat and Wagner. *The English Journal, 86*(4), 78–79.

Weiner, L. (1999). *Urban teaching: The essentials.* New York: Teachers College Press.

Weinstein, C., Curran, M., & Tomlinson-Clarke, S. (2003). Culturally responsive classroom management: Awareness into action. *Theory into Practice, 42*(4), 269–276.

Weissberg, R. P., Durlak, J. A., Domitrovich, C. E., & Gullotta, T. P. (2015). Social and emotional learning: Past, present, and future. In J. A Durlak, C.E. Domitrovich, R. P. Weissberg, & T. P. Gullotta (Eds.), *Handbook of social and emotional learning: Research and practice* (pp. 3–19). New York, NY: Guilford Press.

Wiggins, G., & McTighe, J. (2005). *Understanding by design.* Alexandria, VA: ASCD.

Wiglesworth, M., Lendrum, A., Oldfield, J., Scott, A., ten Bokkel, I., Tate, K., & Emery, C. (2016). The impact of trial stage, developer involvement and international transferability on universal social and emotional learning programme outcomes: A meta-analysis. *Cambridge Journal of Education, 46*(3), 347–376.

Willis, A. I. (2009). EduPolitical research: Reading between the lines. *Educational Researcher. 38*(7), 528–536.

Wlodkowski, R. J., & Ginsberg, M. B. (1995). A framework for culturally responsive teaching. *Educational Leadership, 53*(1), 17–21.

Zeichner, K. (1996). Educating teachers for cultural diversity. In K. Zeichner, S. Melnick, & M. L. Gomez (Eds.), *Currents of reform in preservice teacher education* (pp. 133–175). New York, NY: Teachers College Press.

Index

About the Authors

Christy McConnell, PhD, taught high school English and was department coordinator in Colorado for 7 years. Her master's work focused on teacher preparation and urban education, and her doctoral work explored the practices of ecologically minded teachers. Christy's publications have largely explored aesthetic and ecological perspectives of teaching and learning (she formerly published under the name Moroye). She is now a professor of curriculum studies and educational foundations at the University of Northern Colorado and loves sharing these ideas with her undergraduate and graduate students. Christy spends time in the desert with her son and dogs and enjoys writing poetry, hiking, and running a small art business.

Bradley Conrad, PhD, has been a substitute teacher, high school English teacher, department coordinator, instructional coach, and new teacher mentor during his career beginning in 2001. He earned his MA and PhD in curriculum and instruction from the University of Denver, focusing on culturally responsive teaching, teacher dispositions, and educational policy. He has published work in those areas and is currently the lead on the Tales from the Classroom Project, an undertaking designed to improve education by sharing the voices of those in our schools along with the best research in K–12 education. He is currently an associate professor of education at Capital University in Columbus, Ohio. Bradley is a lifelong Cleveland sports fan who enjoys attending games with his family.

P. Bruce Uhrmacher, PhD, taught in three different alternative high school settings, being responsible not only for teaching social studies, in which he held a credential, but also for much of the extended curriculum including PE, interdisciplinary topics, and art. Currently, Bruce is a professor of research methods as well as curriculum and instruction at the Morgridge College of Education, University of Denver. His publications have focused largely on aesthetic teaching and learning, Waldorf schools, alternative types of schools and curriculum, and a research method called criticism and connoisseurship. Bruce loves music and started drumming when he turned 50.

SUPPLEMENTAL LESSON PLAN AUTHORS

Courtney Berry has been a special education teacher, language arts teacher, instructional coach, administrator, and faculty member in the Denver metro area for students in grades K through 8. Her research interests include multiculturalism, alternative licensure teachers, and teacher preparation.

Meagan Brown is the special education coordinator and a mathematics teacher for a private school in southern California. Her research interests include curriculum theory and practice, multimodality, aesthetic education, and place-based education.

David San Juan is a National Board Certified Teacher with an MA in educational psychology. He has been an elementary school teacher and administrator for 20 years in both public and private schools in the United States and various overseas locations including Spain, India, Egypt, Gaza, and Thailand. David enjoys music, writing, and creating innovative teaching materials for students and teachers. He is currently pursuing his doctorate in educational studies at the University of Northern Colorado.